IDENTITY THEFT

DISCOVERING THE REAL YOU

To: Dr. Smith

May this book inspire and empower you to walk in who you were destined to be. You shall recover ALL!

Thanks for your support!

Love,

DeMonica Gladney

ADVANCE PRAISE ON
IDENTITY THEFT

"The premise for **Identity Theft** is very significant in light of the struggle so many people have with discovering who they are in Christ and living out that relationship through their life! DeMonica's 'investigative' abilities as a lawyer make the analogies even stronger and very insightful. **Identity Theft** is a wonderful book full of powerful, personal testimonies and insightful analogies to help one discover their real 'you' in Christ Jesus!"

Dr. Sonny Foraker
Senior Pastor, First Baptist Church - Pearland
Pearland, TX

"DeMonica Gladney is a dynamite young lady who has a powerful new book that shares strategies and ideas that give you a new perspective on discovering the real you and not letting the real you be stolen away! Read this book, then re-read it, and then share it with your friends! She shows you how the best you, is within you!"

Willie Jolley
Best Selling Author of *A Setback Is A Setup For A Comeback* &
Turn Setbacks Into Greenbacks
Washington, DC

"DeMonica Gladney has provided a divinely inspired path to our true identity. For those willing to take an *honest* journey, she helps uncover areas of "spiritual identity theft" while providing guidance toward God intended authenticity. Her true light and spiritual wisdom shine; blessing those who are willing to receive her literary gifts."

Norma Jarrett-York
Best Selling Author of Inspirational Novels
Sunday Brunch, Sweet Magnolia* & *Sunday Brunch Diaries
Houston, TX

"**Identity Theft** is a powerful tool for evaluating one's stolen identity while reinforcing it. It's a must-read for everyone who desires to discover who they really are from the inside out."

Victor McGlothin
Essence* Bestselling Author of *The Secrets of Newberry
Plano, TX

"***Identity Theft*** is spectacular! No other book combines the spiritual and the natural aspect of identity theft. DeMonica Gladney does an excellent compilation of revealing the spiritual phenomenon of identity theft of a person's total identification. This book is one of DeMonica Gladney's greatest works!"

Shanelle Gilbert, LPC
Author of *Love That Moves Mountains* & *The Wilderness Season*
Choose Life Publications
Humble, TX

"This is a dynamic book that forces you to come face to face with who you are now and the real you God intended. While hopefully they are one and the same, DeMonica Gladney alerts us to the fact that often we, without even knowing it, allow the enemy to steal our true identity inherited from God. In this book, she helps us learn how to recover our identity, walk in our purpose, and live life as God has planned. Congratulations to the author for a well written, timely, and essential message that is both preventative and redemptive. I believe each reader will be blessed."

Troy J. Wilson, Esq.
Pastor, Unity Adventist Worship Center
Houston, TX

"***Identity Theft*** is like an alarm clock going off. It awakens the Body of Christ to the crimes being committed against the believer's experience of all that he or she possesses through Jesus Christ."

Laura Wilcox
Author of *Capture My Heart, Lord*
Houston, TX

"The Holy Spirit leads DeMonica to teach and minister metaphorically by using an analogy, real life experiences, and practical application to help readers understand and know their true identity in Jesus Christ. Satan and his pseudo (fake) cohorts are exposed and people are empowered."

Prophetess Monique Lampkin, MATS
Setting The House In Divine Order Ministries
Houston, TX

"In **Identity Theft**, DeMonica Gladney walks you through the arduous task of rediscovering your emotional, physical, financial and spiritual identity. She artfully reveals the answers to three of life's most important questions: 'Who are you? Where are you going? and What is your destiny?' This book is a manual to help you through your journey of self-discovery. An absolute must-read if you desire to find the *real* you."

Dr. Kervin J. Smith
Author of *The Seven Spirits of A Woman, Your Destiny Now!* &
Overcoming the Enemy Within
Minneapolis, MN

"If you have ever been robbed or experienced theft or loss, you can recall the roll coaster of emotions you felt...fear, betrayal and depression. **Identity Theft** speaks passionately to the hearts and minds of those who have experienced spiritual identity theft. Author DeMonica Gladney gives a practical step-by-step guide to help you identify what has been stolen and how to move toward self-discovery. Through this must-read book, lives will be transformed and true identities discovered."

Dr. Connie Stewart
Author of *The Master Orchestrator*
Life Coach, Life in Bloom
Houston, TX

"If you have struggled with your spiritual relationship, had a problem consistently resisting the devil, or lived your life through the eyes of others, you should read, digest and apply **Identity Theft**. This book will cause you to examine your spiritual relationship with God, confront the enemy within and cause you to reclaim the person God formed you to become. While reading the God inspired word, you will laugh, cry and rejoice. When you are done, you will find that you are stronger, better and wiser than the day you began this spiritual journey."

Pamela J. Meanes, Esq.
Reverend, The New Freedom Baptist Church
Belleville, IL

"In ***Identity Theft: Discovering The Real You***, DeMonica Gladney exposes the enemy for exactly who he is: a liar and a thief. If you wish to take back who you are in Christ, this book is a must-read."

Madeline C. Kirksey
Author of *In Pursuit of the Promise*
Houston, TX

"***Identity Theft*** is a very thought provoking work that captures the heart of God and encourages the readers to take spiritual inventory of their lives. If you have been experiencing a void in your life, ***Identity Theft*** will lead you into a personal encounter with God and place you on the path to discovering who God created you to be from the foundation of the world. I would highly recommend this book to anyone seeking a closer walk with God and the pursuit of their God-given identity!"

Pastor Lasonya M. Stuckey
Author of *Created to Prosper:*
Going From Just Enough to More Than Enough
Seed Planters International Ministry
Baltimore, MD

"So many believers go through life not fulfilling their God-given purpose and their true destiny simply because they don't realize whose they are (children of the Most High God) and don't fully understand the extraordinary significance behind that familial relationship. We cheat ourselves out of becoming who He has created us to become. ***Identity Theft*** brilliantly explores this spiritual 'identity crisis' phenomenon surprisingly prevalent within the Christian community, and encourages readers to re-discover who they are in Christ. It convicts us to better understand that if we are the children of the One who created the universe, then as heirs to His throne, the possibilities for our lives are limitless. What a blessed revelation set forth in such a thoughtful and relatable book! This book has truly been a blessing to me, and I know it will be to you. An absolute must read!"

Evangeline M. Mitchell, Esq.
Author of *Conquering the Bar Exam: Personal Stories and*
Practical Advice for Overcoming the Final Hurdle to
Becoming a Full-Fledged Licensed Lawyer
Houston, TX

IDENTITY THEFT

DISCOVERING THE REAL YOU

DeMonica D. Gladney, Esq.
Bestselling Author of *Willing to Wait*

NEW HORIZON PUBLISHERS
PEARLAND, TEXAS

IDENTITY THEFT: DISCOVERING THE REAL YOU

Copyright © 2011 by DeMonica D. Gladney
All rights reserved.

Unless otherwise noted, scripture references in this book are from the King James Version of the Holy Bible.

No part of this book may be reproduced or transmitted in any form or by any means, electronic or mechanical, including photocopying, recording or storing information in a retrieval system, without prior written permission from the publisher.

Published by:
New Horizon Publishers
8325 Broadway, #202, Box 227
Pearland, TX 77581
Phone: (281) 489-9640
Fax: (281) 489-5044
Email: info@newhorizonpublishers.com
Website: www.newhorizonpublishers.com

Cover Designed by:
Xavier Porter, Injoi MyDesign

ISBN: 978-0-9724229-1-8

Library of Congress Control Number: 2010932583

Printed in the United States of America by
Morris Publishing®
3212 East Hwy 30
Kearney, NE 68847
1-800-650-7888

DEDICATED

To my dear mother,

Dianne Gladney McBride

for her love, support and sacrifice

ACKNOWLEDGEMENTS

To my Heavenly Father, God, who created me in His own image and helped me to discover my "real" identity in Christ. Because of His love for me, I know *who* I am and *whose* I am. To God be the glory!

To my sister, Dr. Connie Stewart, for her encouragement and words of wisdom when I needed them the most, and my brother-in-law, Apostle Joshua Stewart, for his spiritual insight. Thanks for your love and support!

To my nephew, Caleb, and nieces, Cacey and Destiny Stewart, whom I love dearly.

To the staff of New Horizon Publishers for their hard work and commitment to this book project. I love your spirit of excellence!

To Xavier Porter of InJoi MyDesign for the excellent job on my book cover. Continue to let the Lord use you!

To all of my family and friends for their words of encouragement and support of my literary dreams.

TABLE OF CONTENTS

Introduction: *Exposing Identity Theft*..15
Theme Poem: *Stolen Identity* 19

STEP 1 – *Identify What Is Missing*

Chapter 1   Know What You're Looking For 27
Chapter 2   Don't Be Taken By Surprise 41
Chapter 3   What's Really At Risk? 59

STEP 2 – *Inventory The Actual Loss*

Chapter 4   Don't Let Your Guards Down 79
Chapter 5   The Search To Find "You" 99
Chapter 6   In Pursuit Of Your Purpose 121

STEP 3 – *Inspect All The Findings*

Chapter 7   Check Out Your Sources 139
Chapter 8   Check All Your Pockets 157
Chapter 9   Target The Real Enemy 179

STEP 4 – *Initiate The Full Recovery*

Chapter 10   On The Road To Recovery 201
Chapter 11   Go Get The "Real You" Back 213
Chapter 12   Walk Into The "New" 225

LIST OF TABLES

Table 1   Four Steps To Recover Your Stolen Identity 21

Table 2   The Key Sources of Your Identity 156

Table 3   The 3P's Connected To Your Stolen Identity 177

Table 4   Indictment of Satan For Spiritual Identity Theft 212

INTRODUCTION
Exposing Identity Theft

Imagine finding out that someone has been posing as you for days, weeks or even months. Since you know that the imposter is not you, shouldn't it be just as easy for others to figure out the truth? It is not the fault of the stores that gave the imposter merchandise, the banks that handed out money or the creditors that extended credit to the "fake" you. They believed that the thief was you since he or she apparently had proper identification to prove it. After the thief had maxed out the fraudulent credit cards in your name and left the bills or loans unpaid, these same businesses now want you to assume your "stolen" identity and pay up. Sadly, this sounds like another tragic case of "identity theft."

Despite all the efforts to combat identity theft, it has become the fastest growing crime in America. Almost ten million people fall victim to this "faceless" crime in the United States each year. Identity theft is an equal opportunity crime, affecting victims of all races, ages and income levels. It occurs when someone obtains and uses your personal identifying information (e.g., name, date of birth, social security or credit card number) for personal gain. This serious crime can happen in a variety of ways, such as when a thief steals your credit card to make purchases, impersonates you to open a loan, pretends to be you when arrested for a crime or even uses your social security number to apply for a job. Since there is no one-size fits all when it comes to identity theft, we must figure out how to protect ourselves from a moving target.

Identity theft works best when the unsuspecting victims remain unaware of what has happened. Many people don't even realize that their identity has been stolen until it's too late. They only discover their plight once their credit has been ruined, and they have suffered substantial, financial losses. I know first-hand because it happened to me about seven years ago. I didn't discover the theft until almost three months after it happened. Before I could stop the impersonator, she had already maxed out all of the new credit cards that had been fraudulently opened. Since she didn't have a driver's license in my name to "officially" pose as me, she decided to use my social security number along with her own personal information. Since the retailers apparently didn't notice the discrepancy, I was left holding the bag with nearly $10,000 in bills for merchandise, like computers, printers, tires and clothes that I had never seen. Moreover, I later discovered a fraudulent mortgage loan in my name for a $1.3 million house. I was shocked and appalled that the thief was able to use my "identity" to obtain more luxuries than I had using my own identity.

Although I had taken proactive steps to protect myself, I still ended up becoming a "victim" of identity theft. I was very careful about giving out my personal information. I checked my credit reports and reviewed my bank statements in a timely manner. I was devastated because there was nothing else I could have done to avoid this essentially "virtual" crime. It was not as if the thief had physically taken anything from me or stolen my social security card. My purse was not stolen, my credit cards were not lost, and my debit card personal identification number (PIN) was not misused. However, this predator was actually a pickpocket and had effectively slipped my identity right out of my pocket without me knowing it.

While I was fighting to recover my stolen identity, I was forced into a complicated legal battle to prove that I

Introduction: Exposing Identity Theft

didn't make any of the fraudulent transactions. While the identity thief got the benefit of the doubt with my identity, I was treated as if I were the criminal instead of the victim. When I came to the realization that neither the police, the federal agencies, the prosecutor nor the creditors could help me to bring the culprit to justice, I decided to investigate my own identity theft case. In fact, I had to gather all the evidence to give to the police before they would even pursue my case.

While I was still struggling with my ordeal, I recalled how often I had heard the expression, "First natural, then spiritual." If this type of identity theft was happening in the natural, I wondered what the enemy had been up to behind the scenes in the spiritual realm. Then, I imagined going through life and suddenly discovering that my "spiritual identity" had been stolen. This thought led me to the scripture, *John 10:10*, which states that the thief comes to <u>steal</u>, kill and destroy. That's when I knew that I had also been exposed to "spiritual identity theft," which is even more traumatic and life-altering than the loss of my money and credit. Spiritual identity theft occurs when Satan slowly and subtly tries to steal our sense of who we are and leaves us searching for our purpose and destiny.

When the Lord first gave me the book title, *Identity Theft: Discovering the Real You*, I didn't fully know what He wanted me to share with you. As a victim of natural and spiritual identity theft, I have experienced the damaging effects of losing my identity in two ways. As a result, I finally realized that with the same tenacity that I went after the imposter who stole my "natural" identity, I had to go after the identity thief in the "spiritual" realm. That's why it's so important that spiritual identity theft be exposed for what it really is...a deceptive scheme of Satan to rob us of our God-given identity.

Similar to the natural crime, many victims of spiritual identity theft may not even be aware of what has happened until it's too late. This kind of spiritual theft may go unaddressed for many years until you face a difficult situation, such as a divorce, a bad relationship, the death of a loved one, the loss of a job, a chronic illness or a financial struggle, and end up having to do a personal inventory of your life. At that point, you suddenly discover that your spiritual identity has been stolen or lost in the process, and you end up asking yourself the critical question, "Who am I?" Only then can you begin the long and challenging, but necessary journey in search of your spiritual identity. It's the only way that you can finally discover and reclaim the "real" you.

In *Identity Theft,* the discussion on how to recover your stolen identity is divided into four essential steps (see Table 1):

   Step 1 – Identify What Is Missing
   Step 2 – Inventory The Actual Loss
   Step 3 – Inspect All The Findings
   Step 4 – Initiate The Full Recovery

This book will walk you step by step through your own spiritual identity theft case, so that you can identify and recover everything that the enemy has stolen from you. As you begin your personal journey of self-discovery, be prepared to fight for what rightfully belongs to you...your "spiritual identity."

THEME POEM
Stolen Identity

I did not know my identity was at risk,
While I was going through life in total bliss,
All of a sudden my ID was just stolen away,
But I couldn't narrow it down to a specific day,
Well it could have been when I failed my test,
Or when I was told to be better than the rest,
Sometime between my childhood and now,
I had lost myself, but didn't fully know how,
From the outside, everything looked fine,
But the face I saw in the mirror wasn't mine,
I began a long journey in search of me,
Yet who I really was, I could no longer see,
I had somehow lost sight of the "real" me,
Blinded by my past and filled with insecurity,
I was not sure about my true self-worth,
Or for what purpose I was put on this earth,
Like everyone else I wanted to be affirmed,
But I was taken advantage of at every turn,
I had been robbed by bad relationships,
And those who loved only with their lips,
The enemy wanted me to feel ashamed,
And to focus on someone else to blame,
Then I started to really question who I am,
Feeling very pressured and overwhelmed,
My good name was secretly taken from me,
And it left me as devastated as I can be,
But it didn't compare to what came next,
When I could not put my life into context,
All of those missing pieces that I lacked,
I had to take steps to get them all back,

Stolen Identity (con't)

But I didn't want to remember the past,
Yet I wasn't ready to take off my mask,
I had lost all my confidence and worth,
And just couldn't let go of all the hurt;
A head-on collision tried to take me out,
Bringing even more fear and self-doubt,
I had been living my life for everyone else,
And not having any quality time for myself,
I was driven to succeed by all that was said,
And did what was needed to get ahead,
A real perfectionist through and through,
My self-esteem became tied to what I do,
How it all happened I did not have a clue,
And the trials I went through were not few,
But I knew that I was a threat to the enemy,
That's why he didn't want me to know "me,"
I had been struggling to find the right way,
And always worried about what people say,
Yet God knew me in my mother's womb,
So my God-given identity I could assume,
Now that I know what He said about me,
From others' opinions I am now finally free,
I had to fight to get my true identity back,
And follow the Truth instead of the facts,
The enemy came to steal, kill and destroy,
But when Jesus came he didn't get very far,
So now I can start living the abundant life,
For I know that my "real" identity is in Christ,
Now I finally know who I was created to be,
But first I had to reclaim my "stolen identity."

Copyright © June 2010 by DeMonica D. Gladney

TABLE 1
Four Steps To Recover Your Stolen Identity

STEPS	NATURAL THEFT	SPIRITUAL THEFT
STEP 1 **Identity What Is Missing**	Confirm if your *natural* identity (e.g., name, social security no.) has been stolen	Confirm if your *spiritual* identity (i.e., who you are in Christ) has been stolen or lost
STEP 2 **Inventory The Actual Loss**	Create a list of the *natural* things that you believe were stolen (e.g., credit, money)	Create a list of the *spiritual* things that you believe were stolen or lost (e.g., purpose, destiny)
STEP 3 **Inspect All The Findings**	Review the *facts* (e.g., reports) closely to determine what was actually stolen (e.g., good name)	Review the *truth* (i.e., Bible) closely to determine what was actually stolen (e.g., character)
STEP 4 **Initiate The Full Recovery**	Take *legal* action to get your natural identity back (e.g., file police report, go to court)	Take *spiritual* action to get your spiritual identity back (e.g., go to the Supreme Judge)

STEP 1

IDENTIFY
What Is Missing

"You will know that your tent is secure; you will take stock of your property and find nothing **missing**."

Job 5:24 (NIV)

POETIC EXHORTATION
What Is Missing

I have to identify what is missing,

So to get started I had to go fishing,

Searching through the pieces of my life,

That's when I was forced to look twice,

To figure out what happened to "me,"

So I could recover my stolen identity.

STEP 1
Overview

The first step in the process of recovering your stolen identity is to <u>identify</u> what is missing in your life. During this step, you have to confirm if something is in fact missing before you can determine what has happened to your identity. If you are not aware that anything is missing, you won't know that you need to look for "it." I used to have a unique, college ring that I kept in my jewelry box to make sure I didn't lose it. One day when I decided to wear it, I discovered that it was missing. I was unsure if someone had stolen it or if I had somehow lost or misplaced it. Regardless of how or when it disappeared, I now knew that my ring was missing and had to figure out what happened to it. As a result, I went on a long rampage to try to find it. Once I had identified what was missing, I knew exactly what I was looking for.

However, if you don't know that your identity has been stolen, you won't even bother to look for it. For example, if you buy a jigsaw puzzle, you assume that all the pieces are in the box. Only after you start trying to put the puzzle together do you realize that one or more of the pieces are missing. At that point, you may check the box to see if any of the pieces were left inside. If you don't find the missing pieces, you will never be able to put the entire puzzle together. You may experience the same problem if you are unaware that your identity is missing. You may assume that your identity is intact until you discover that it is gone while trying to put the pieces of your life together. Once you know or have a suspicion that your identity has been stolen, you must figure out specifically what is missing in order to get it back.

REFLECTIONS ON
Identity Theft

"Americans are more worried about becoming a victim of Identity Theft than getting laid off..."
 Wayne Abernathy, Asst. U.S. Treasury Secretary,
 ***USA Today* 2003**

"I don't need to worry about identity theft because no one wants to be me."
 Jay London

Chapter 1

Know What You're Looking For

Before we can even address the issue of "identity theft," we need to understand the "crisis" that has been going on with our identities. A "crisis" refers to an emotionally stressful event or traumatic change in a person's life. We constantly hear about the economic crisis, the housing crisis, the banking crisis, the health care crisis, and recently the oil spill crisis in the Gulf, but no one is talking about the "identity crisis" that we all have experienced at some point in our lives. The term, "identity crisis," is a psychological term, which describes someone who is in a constant state of searching for his or her identity. The person may be at a major turning point or crossroad in his or her life and struggling with who he or she is. During that process, the person is basically trying to figure out what is missing in his or her life. However, before the person can even deal with the identity crisis, he or she must know what he or she is looking for in the midst of the crisis.

In Crisis Mode

Some people aren't able to function in their daily lives if they are not in a crisis mode. We're so accustomed to dealing with crisis after crisis with our spouses, kids, jobs, finances or health that such stress becomes acceptable to us. We plug one hole and another one opens up, which is the only reason we do anything different than the norm. Not until we experience a real crisis situation will we start thinking about making changes in our lives. I think it's human nature to wait until things get bad before we decide to take action, rather than addressing the problem when it first arises. Many of us take the same approach when we struggle with our identities. We may become confused or uncertain about who we are, but we tend to overlook those concerns until it gets to a crisis level. It just takes one challenging situation to force us to question who we are.

We live in a world full of people who are walking around feeling lost, but they may not even know it or know what to do about it. Sometimes, many of us don't feel as if we fit into various aspects of our lives...at home, at work, at school or at church. It's similar to trying to fit a square peg into a round hole. We may be searching for a sense of belonging to someone or something, so in line with the old expression, we have learned to "get in where we fit in." We don't want to be different or unique because we're too busy trying to blend in with the crowd. Whether we feel comfortable or not, we will connect with people or situations where we can receive affirmation or validation without even realizing it. During times of self-doubt, many of us are simply experiencing an identity crisis. We don't know who we are or why we are here. We have lost our "real" identity along the way, but we may not have been aware of it because we're in a crisis mode.

When we're going through an identity crisis, it's not unusual for us to be confused about who we are. I remember experiencing this type of crisis when I started college, which should have been the best time of my life. However, I was still recovering from a near fatal car accident, which was one of the most traumatic experiences in my life. I was dealing with the insecurities that came with the loss of my voice, but I didn't fully know how deeply I had been affected in other ways until much later. I can't pinpoint exactly when it happened, but I slowly began to struggle with my identity. Since I began to question who I really was, I found myself trying to fit in with the popular crowd. I felt like I was the only one going through an identity crisis. On top of that, I was so stressed out that I went through a period of insomnia during my last semester of college. When I went to the doctor, I was shocked by the diagnosis: I was depressed. I didn't know exactly what was missing in my life, but at that point, I finally recognized the internal conflict that I had been dealing with. However, I had been trying to confront my situation from a natural perspective when it was actually a "spiritual identity crisis."

Many Christians are constantly in and out of a spiritual identity crisis. We may actually find ourselves confused about who we are from a spiritual perspective. Some of us may have allowed people to tell us who we are, whether good or bad, our entire lives, so that we don't know for ourselves. In fact, we can sometimes forget who we really are and lose sight of our spiritual identity as a result. The person who we have become may be further and further away from who God actually created us to be. That's why we can feel close to God one moment, and then feel distant from Him the next. We may even have days of great spiritual victories followed by periods of major, natural defeats.

After the prophet Elijah had miraculously called down fire from heaven and destroyed the 450 prophets of Baal, he experienced this same type of spiritual identity crisis (*1 Kings 18*). He soon thereafter found himself in a cave hiding from Jezebel. Sometime between his great victory over his enemies and his visit to the cave, he began to question his own identity, experiencing a spiritual identity crisis. Likewise, many of us have gone through a similar type of crisis even though we know who we were called to be.

As believers, we should know that we're the children of God, joint-heirs with Christ, a chosen generation and a royal priesthood. However, we can still experience a spiritual identity crisis. When our faith is challenged or we have a major loss in our lives, we may begin to wonder, "Who am I?" Many of us are struggling with our identities, whether or not we are willing to admit it. From the outside, I appeared to have it "all" together years after I had recuperated from my car accident. At least this was the perception that people, including my family and friends, had of me. However, I felt completely different on the inside and knew that something was still missing in my life. I couldn't specifically identify what was wrong, but I knew that something was off. It's one thing to know you have a problem, but it's another thing to be able to identify what it is. If you know the diagnosis, then you can get to the prognosis. The reason that we don't know that pieces of our identity are missing is because we have been secretly ripped off by the master pickpocket, Satan, while we were going through our spiritual identity crisis.

Once you determine that something is missing in your life, you need to know what you're looking for. In other words, you need to be sure that you're identifying the "right" problem. The only thing worse than knowing there's a problem is misidentifying it. On the TV show, *House*, Dr. House usually initially misidentifies the patient's condition and starts treating him or her for the wrong illness. He keeps going through his "diagnosis list" until he figures out the "real" problem, and most of the patients fully recover once their condition is properly treated. His approach to practicing medicine may not be very conventional, but he does try to rule out the wrong thing to get to the right thing. That's exactly what needs to happen when our spiritual identities are missing. We have to keep searching until we can correctly identify the right problem, so we can properly address our spiritual identity crisis.

A Case of Spiritual Amnesia

After we understand our spiritual identity crisis, we are on the right road to recovering our God-given identities. However, we have to first determine if we have a case of spiritual amnesia. Amnesia may involve a partial or total loss of a person's memory, usually immediately following some type of trauma. The amnesia can have a short-term or long-term impact depending on the severity of the injury. A person may receive some kind of blunt force trauma to the head and wake up feeling fine, even functioning normally. However, the person doesn't know who he or she is anymore. When I had my head-on collision, I had a major blow to my head. I was hit with so much force that my head put a hole in the windshield. After being knocked unconscious, I remained in my car for over four hours until the police arrived. Despite the lacerations to my face and the hole in my throat, I was otherwise physically fine. However, I suffered from partial amnesia and initially could only recall what happened right before the point of impact. The experience was so distressing that my mind had subconsciously blocked it out. The same thing can happen when we go through a difficult or painful situation in our lives, pushing our minds to block out the trauma as if it never happened.

Many of us have life experiences similar to Jason Bourne in the movie, *The Bourne Identity*. He suffered from severe amnesia, which left him frustrated about who he was. Jason had been brainwashed and had no idea who he was or why he was in a particular location or situation. In turn, he went on a never-ending pursuit to discover his real identity. Our lives may not be as dramatic, but our questions are the same as his: "Who am I, and why am I here?" Consequently, we run from job to job, relationship to relationship or even church to church, trying to "find" ourselves.

Similarly, many Christians are going through life as if they truly know who they are, but they're really suffering from spiritual amnesia. It's like they woke up one day and discovered that they didn't know who they were spiritually. Spiritual amnesia occurs when someone is confused about whom God created them to be and who they have actually become. It's a real tragedy for believers to have that kind of amnesia, where they struggle with who they really are. They may not have a total memory loss, but just enough to forget their identity in Christ. In turn, they go back and forth about who they are. So one day they are "the head," and then the next day they are "the tail." They are "above," and then they are suddenly "beneath." They may see themselves as more than a conqueror (Romans 8:37), and then the next minute they feel like a complete failure. These amnesia victims may oscillate like a fan because remember they are still going through a spiritual identity crisis and have become double minded.

"A double minded man is unstable in all his ways."
James 1:8

As a result, they have a "divided" mind and are unbalanced in everything they do. However, it doesn't have to be this way if they can remember who they really are in Christ. Has this type of identity tug of war happened to you or someone you know?

If we have amnesia and don't know who we are, it's so easy for us to simply rely on what people tell us. If you lose your memory, the doctor may ask you, "Do you remember your name?" If your answer is "no," then your family and friends may try to help jog your memory by telling you things about yourself that will help you recall. However, no matter how much they tell you, it's usually futile until you actually remember for yourself. It could be months or years before you get your memory back. In the meantime, you have to rely on what everyone else says about you. I can tell you from personal experience that it's a horrible feeling to not know who you are and have to rely on others to introduce you to yourself.

People may also try to take advantage of us when we suffer from amnesia. When I was still recuperating from my car accident, the drunk driver who almost killed me served me with a $1 million lawsuit. The police officer on my case later sent me a handwritten note in the mail stating that I was at fault and had told him at the scene that I fell asleep. However, that could not be true: I was unable to talk at that time, so the judge dismissed the ticket. As you can see, he tried to take advantage of my memory loss, but it backfired. When you have amnesia, people who you never expect to hurt you will try to use your loss against you.

If you do suffer from spiritual amnesia, you must be careful because the people closest to you can shape your perception of who you are, rightly or wrongly. If you don't know who you are and people tell you that you're a failure, a mistake, a loser or an embarrassment, you may believe them and start acting like who they say you are. As a result, you have to be very cautious about who you allow to speak into your life because words can have a lasting impact on you. The old adage, "sticks and stones may break your bones, but words will never hurt you" is the biggest lie. Not only can words hurt you, they can destroy you if you let them.

> "Death and life are in the power of the tongue: and they that love it shall eat the fruit thereof."
> *Proverbs 18:21*

Words do have power and can be used to speak life or death to you and others. I recall several times when people have said things about me that weren't true, but I would try to just ignore them without saying anything. For example, I had a healthy appetite when I was a teenager, and my stepfather used to constantly say that I was going to be "big as a house" when I got older. I would pretend to laugh about it, but his words really bothered me. In fact, I later realized that a negative seed have been planted in my mind and began to affect my thoughts about myself. So, now if someone tries to say anything that I know is not true about me, I boldly tell him or her, "I don't receive it!"

We have to learn to shut down every word spoken to us that doesn't line up with what God says about us. We have to allow untrue words to fall on deaf ears.

Some cases of spiritual amnesia may be more severe than others. Regardless of the extent of your amnesia, you need to address it because what you think about yourself has a big impact on your behavior. If you think you're a child of God, you should act like you are. If you think you're just a sinner saved by grace, you will act like a sinner. A good biblical example is the story of the Israelites, who were treated like slaves in Egypt for so long that they started to think and act as if they were actually slaves. Although God kept trying to remind them that they were destined to be a great nation, they still didn't know who they were. The Israelites were God's chosen people, but at times they wanted to return to Egypt rather than go through their testing in the wilderness. They murmured and complained wanting to turn back to a familiar place of bondage. That's the epitome of a spiritual identity crisis. How can people chosen by God not know who they are? God was in their midst, yet they still suffered from spiritual amnesia. Similar to believers today who suffer from spiritual amnesia, their problems stemmed from their worldly thinking. It was the very crisis with their identity that kept causing them to stumble, and as a result, many of them never made it to the Promised Land.

The plight of the Israelites is far different from the story of Joseph, the son of Jacob, who was sold into slavery by his brothers. Despite everything he experienced after he told them his dream about his family bowing down to him, he still knew who he was. He went from the pit to the palace, and then to prison when he was falsely accused by Potipher's wife. No matter how difficult his situation became, he never wavered in his trust in God or his perception of who God had called him to be. Not once did he think of himself as a slave or act like one. He never allowed his circumstances to dictate who he was. Because Joseph had not forgotten who he was, he was able to hold on to his spiritual identity and fulfill his divine purpose.

Likewise, if we want to hold onto our spiritual identities, we must take steps to avoid spiritual amnesia. We must never forget that we are only "in" the world, not "of" the world. We need to realize that we are actually "spirit" beings living out a natural existence, rather than "natural" beings living out a spiritual one. That's why the Bible tells us to be "spiritually" minded because that's the only way we can stay connected to who we were created to be by God.

I recall a powerful song, *There Is a King in You*, by Donald Lawrence, which addresses this very issue. He reminds believers that we come from royalty, and there is a King (the King of kings) in us. If we really believe that we have a King in us, how can we not know who we are? If our Father is the King, we are royalty and should act like it. The song goes on to say that, "The goal of the enemy is that you don't know who you are." This is so true. No matter what you've gone through in the past or are currently going through, there is a King in you. Unlike many of us, people who are royalty know who they are and what they are entitled to. Despite whatever you've gone through - the divorce, the abuse, the addiction, the cancer, the failure, etc. - it does not change who you are in Christ. It's up to you to do whatever it takes to get your spiritual memory back, so you can end your spiritual identity crisis.

Get Back To Eden

We must understand man's identity before the fall in order to fully comprehend our current spiritual identity crisis. If we know how God views us, it becomes the basis for how we view ourselves. The search for who we are began long ago in the Garden of Eden. We have to get back to that same garden to see exactly where we fit into God's creation. The Bible is clear that man was created in the image of God (Genesis 1:27). Since we were created in His image, we should look like Him and have His character. He blessed man and gave him dominion over the earth and every living creature.

> "Then God blessed them, and God said to them, be fruitful and multiply; fill the earth and subdue it; have dominion over the fish of the sea, over the birds of the air, and over every living thing that moves on the earth."
>
> *Genesis 1:28*

In the Garden of Eden, Adam and Eve were never deprived, and they were totally connected to and dependent on God. Their lives in the garden were literally "heaven on earth," and they were living on top of the world. It was a time in which man was complete and whole as God intended from the beginning. However, there was an adversary just waiting for Adam and Eve to mess up, so he could put an end to their loving relationship with God. There was no bondage or sin in the Garden of Eden until the spiritual identity thief, Satan, showed up to tempt them. It was not until after their fall that Adam and Eve became aware of their nakedness and hid from God. At that point, they slowly began to go through their own spiritual identity crisis.

After all was said and done, Adam and Eve were struggling to get back to the place that God had originally intended for them. There is another song, *Back II Eden*, by Donald Lawrence that is right on point. The song states, "Let's get back to Eden, live on top of the world." It reminds us that our families, our finances, our minds, our spirits and our bodies are blessed, and we have to keep telling ourselves how blessed we are. I think Lawrence is simply telling us to remember who God created us to be when we start suffering from spiritual amnesia. If we focus only on the fact that the tempter (Satan) came to interfere with God's plan for man, then we will live beneath our privileges as children of God. Adam and Eve did fall, but that was not the end of the story. After they fell, Jesus came to make everything well. As believers, we can confidently say that "all is well." It may not look well or feel well, but all things work together for our good.

> "And we know that all things work together for good to them that love God, to them who are the called according to his purpose."
>
> *Romans 8:28*

Even if our situation itself is not good, God will still work all things together for our ultimate good. He allows everything that we're going through, good and bad, to be used to fulfill His purpose in our lives. We must realize that God divinely orchestrates every aspect of our lives and knows the part that we play in His overall plan. This is the insightful premise that my sister, Dr. Connie Stewart, highlights in her book, *The Master Orchestrator*. She reaffirms that "God is working even in the darkest hours of our lives and that His hand is always moving! Even when we can't see His face!" With this powerful insight, we all need to "get back to Eden" and start living on top of the world. Are you living on top of the world where you should be? Or are you somewhere near the bottom? Only you can be the judge.

King David is a great biblical example of someone who could have suffered from spiritual amnesia, but instead chose to get back to Eden to understand who he was. We need to join him in his bold declaration to God in *Psalm 139*.

> "...I will praise thee; for I am fearfully and wonderfully made: marvellous are thy works; and that my soul knoweth right well."
> *Psalm 139:14*

We are also fearfully and wonderfully made and should know by now exactly who we are. Even when we are suffering from spiritual amnesia, God knows who we are and why we are here. It's up to us to allow Him to reveal who He created us to be and to also walk fully in who we are in Christ.

Another lesson that we can learn from the Garden of Eden is that Satan, who desires to steal our spiritual identity, does so by playing mind games. That's why it's so important for us to keep our minds stayed on the Lord.

> "Thou wilt keep him in perfect peace, whose mind is stayed on thee: because he trusteth in thee."
> *Isaiah 26:3*

The apostle Paul warned the Corinthians that the same serpent who deceived Eve in the garden is the same one who wanted to trick them.

> "But I fear, lest by any means, as the serpent beguiled Eve through his subtilty, so your minds should be corrupted from the simplicity that is in Christ."
>
> *2 Corinthians 11:3*

Paul knew that the serpent had no control over Adam and Eve's situation, but he could try to gain access to their minds in order to steal their identities. Paul was referring back to when they were in the Garden of Eden. As long as they stayed in the presence of God, the serpent could not touch them. However, Eve was ultimately deceived into eating the forbidden fruit. Once she started listening to Satan, she opened the door for him to start messing with her mind. It wasn't long before she went from just thinking about the fruit to eating it, and then Adam joined right in. They had no idea that they were being robbed blind by the spiritual identity thief or the extent of the loss they would suffer from disobeying God. Now, we can see why they began to suffer a spiritual identity crisis.

Likewise, it's no surprise why we find ourselves experiencing the same type of spiritual crisis that occurred in the Garden of Eden. When Adam and Eve were living on top of the world, they still struggled with who God created them to be. As believers, we may be going through a similar struggle and asking the question, "Who am I?" That's the question we should be able to answer unless we have spiritual amnesia. We have already gone back to the garden to examine this issue, but we need to take a closer look at it so the enemy won't take us by surprise.

Chapter 2

Don't Be Taken By Surprise

After we realize the extent of our spiritual identity crisis, we need to understand what "identity theft" really means. Picture a woman walking out of a store alone after dark on Christmas Eve and pushing the remote to unlock her car. From out of nowhere, two men in a car with the lights out slowly pull up on the side of her. One man snatches her purse while the other one speeds away. They get away with her purse, wallet, money, credit cards and driver's license in one full swoop. It sounds like a scene out of a horror movie, but it actually happened to my friend a couple of years ago. This type of violent crime gets the police's attention, but they can't do anything about it if the victim can't identify the thief, the getaway car doesn't have any license plates or the store's surveillance cameras don't work.

However, I think there may come a time when this type of "face-to-face" crime will only be in the movies. Why would anyone bother to rob or carjack a person when they can simply use a computer to steal a person's entire identity to obtain money, credit cards, loans, and employment?

By now, we all know exactly what "identity theft" is and how it happens. Or do we? Identity theft is one of the most diverse crimes in America, and each case is different. Many Americans never think about identity theft or believe it can happen to them until it finally does. However, recent statistics paint a different picture. Identity theft has topped the Federal Trade Commission's (FTC) list of consumer complaints for the past eight years. A 2009 survey shows that a record 9.9 million Americans were victims of identity theft in 2008, which is a shocking 22% increase over prior years according to Javelin Strategy & Research (Javelin). These statistics confirm that identity theft has reached epidemic proportions and will most likely continue to rise.

In the past few years, there has been considerable concern about identity theft and countless stories about this horrible crime. Every time you turn on the television, there's another news headline about an identity theft ring or corporate hackers being busted or one of the funny commercials showing an elderly woman with the voice of a man who stole her identity. Even our bank or credit card statements now include offers for credit monitoring services to minimize the risk of identity theft. Insurance companies are also offering identity theft insurance coverage, which was unheard of even five years ago. Paper shredders are now much more popular as we become more aware of how important it is to destroy any documents with our sensitive information. Because identity theft is so prevalent now, we need to understand exactly what it is and how it happens. Otherwise, we will be caught off guard and taken by surprise when it occurs.

A thief commits "identity theft" if he or she uses or possesses a person's identifying information without permission with the intent to do harm. A person's "identity" includes his or her name and other key personal data, such as a date of birth, social security number, driver's license number and credit card number. Technically, a thief can steal someone's identifying information without committing identity fraud. For example, a crook could hack into a company's database and access its employees' personal information, but not get to use it if he or she is caught first. The thief's access of the information alone is a crime. However, typically, a thief steals someone's identity and uses it to open bank or credit card accounts in that person's name, and then goes on a spending spree.

Many of you, or someone you know, have experienced some form of identity theft, even as simple as someone stealing your credit or debit card. Identity thieves may obtain a credit card, rent an apartment or set up a telephone account in your name. You may not find out about the theft until you review your credit report or credit card statement and notice charges you didn't make or until you're contacted by a creditor or collection agency.

In my identity theft case, my mortgage company informed me of the suspicious activity on my credit report, and then I had to take immediate action. Otherwise, I may not have found out about the theft until I got my annual credit report the next year, giving the thief ample time to do substantial damage to my name and credit. I point this out because these criminals are no longer just after your money -- they want to actually be you.

You've Been Duplicated

Just over a decade ago, we heard more about the "old-fashioned" type of theft, where the thieves simply stole your electronics and rushed to the pawn shop to sell them for quick cash, than the crime of identity theft. Back then, thieves were more focused on taking your personal property and could care less about your "identity."

I remember when my first designer purse was stolen in high school after a class break. I stepped out of the room for a few minutes, and my purse was gone when I returned. I asked if anyone had seen it, but supposedly no one did. I was very upset and suspicious of everyone who was trying to console me because I knew any one of them could have been the thief. Apparently, my tears must have touched the real thief because the contents of my purse magically showed up in the girl's restroom later that day. The thief only wanted the money and the purse and decided to dump everything else out. This experience was devastating to me, but it was no comparison to the vicious crime of identity theft.

During these tough economic times, thieves have changed their motivation when it comes to getting what they want. So, the real question becomes what do these predators really want from us? They are no longer just after your purse, wallet or jewels, but he or she wants to be you. Not only do they want access to your personal information to steal your "identity," they want to actually become you. Believe it or not, someone wants to be you if only to get access to your stuff. These thieves used to be satisfied with finding a credit card on the ground and buying as much stuff as they could before you cancelled the card. However, now they desire to assume your identity at least temporarily to open up new credit card or bank accounts. They get what they want, and then ditch your identity and leave you with the tarnished version of it. Since the identity thieves can't get the things they want being themselves, they have decided to become someone else who can give them access to those things. That's why a thief will go through a lot of trouble to become you. If you haven't figured it out yet, identity theft simply means that "You've been duplicated!" There are now two of you, the "fake" you and the "real" you, and that's why the creditors are so confused. They don't know which one of you to believe.

When my identity was stolen, the thief took over some of my existing credit card accounts. When I contacted my credit card company to inform them of my identity theft, I was told that the account was not mine, even though I had the credit card in my wallet. Since the imposter's name was now tied to my social security number, the company relied on her name to decide that I was the "fake" me. The representative even threatened to report me to the police if I called back. I was furious and insulted that I didn't get the benefit of the doubt with my own identity. There was definitely something wrong with this picture. Not only was it frustrating to know that someone was posing as me, but also that it was up to me to prove it.

You're probably wondering why identity theft can continue to go on unnoticed even when more and more people are aware of it. The thief's greatest weapon is the element of surprise, and he or she capitalizes on a victim's lack of awareness of the crime. We must understand the difference between theft and robbery if we want to grasp why identify theft has become such a popular crime. "Theft" means to steal something secretly. A thief is usually behind the scenes, waiting to covertly take your valuables without your knowledge. You've heard of the proverbial thief who dresses in black to conceal himself or herself from the targeted victim, so he or she can sneak up on the person. On the contrary, a robber openly takes your stuff by force or the threat of force, and he or she may even hold a gun to your head and say, "This is a stick up...give me all of your money."

Unlike traditional theft, a robbery is a face-to-face confrontation where you know exactly what is stolen and when it's stolen. The term "rob" is widely, but incorrectly, used to refer to theft. For example, people will say that their house was robbed while they were away, but the house was actually burglarized, which is a form of theft. With the many technology advances, an identity thief doesn't even have to go to your house or bank to steal your money or valuables anymore. Since identity theft is a virtual crime, the thief no longer has to physically take anything, come onto your property or compromise your computer to steal your identity. In reality, identity theft is like you walking down a dark street alone and getting mugged by a thief, but you don't know it until weeks later.

All that a predator needs is access to your personal information to steal your identity and start living your life. I knew a so-called doctor who appeared to have a successful medical career. He was always talking about his rounds with patients at the hospital. One day, I turned on the news and heard that he'd been arrested for impersonating another doctor. It took a while before they caught him because he was definitely looking the part with a hospital badge, a white lab jacket and a stethoscope. In fact, the "fake" doctor never even finished his first year of college, but he had actually sat through medical school classes as if he was enrolled. It's amazing that he was able to get access to the medical school, the hospital and the patients for a long time before anyone figured it out. It's frightening that we don't know if the person right next to us is actually the person we think he or she is, so be alert because that same person may be pretending to be you.

Now that you know the perpetrators are after your identity, you can start taking steps to protect it. You can take comfort in the old saying that you can be "imitated, but never duplicated." As much as the identity thief may want to be you, he or she will never actually be you. There is only one "real" you, and you are on an interesting journey to find out who that is. At times, this journey can be frustrating and overwhelming, but at other times it can be very enlightening. It's a process, and you will make it through no matter how difficult it may seem to be right now. You could already be a victim of identity theft and not know that a thief has access to your "numbers."

Who's Got Your Number?

As any identity theft victim can tell you, your identity is one of your most valuable assets. If someone steals your identity to commit fraud, it can affect every aspect of your life – your credit score, your ability to buy a car or house, or even get a job or medical care - and it can take years to repair the damage. Most importantly, it can happen to any of us in ways that we never imagined. An identity thief may already have access to your "numbers" and taken steps to steal your identity, so you better get prepared to deal with it.

In today's hi-tech world, a criminal can steal a person's identity from next door or another country without ever knowing who the victim is. The thief is only concerned with the numbers in a victim's credit report, which are the same numbers that matter to a creditor or lender. These numbers have come to represent our identities. Although a person's good name used to be determined by their integrity and character, now a person's worth is determined by one number, a FICO score. Based on this one number generated by a computer, a person's entire credit worth can be quantified. Moreover, creditors and lenders don't see us as people any more, but as numbers on a computer printout. Identity theft is on the rise, not only because it is relatively easy to commit, but because our society has turned us into numbers. It's easy to strike against a number. Of course, a faceless crime that does not require looking a victim in the eyes is much easier to commit.

When thieves seek to steal your "identity," what does that actually mean? This term, "identity," can be misleading because it can mean both a person and a thing. While "identity" refers to who a person is, it also means something that establishes who the person is, such as a signature, a photo or an identification card. When it comes to identity theft, it's the latter meaning that is usually intended. When a thief steals your personal identifying information, he or she by definition has stolen your "identity." However, what about who a person is on the inside? Can that aspect of his or her "identity" actually be stolen? Since it is intangible, it is technically impossible for it to be physically stolen. While the identity thief may steal your personal information for his or her financial gain, he or she can't actually steal your "real" identity. Sadly, you just cease living from and enjoying the benefits of your true identity. An imposter can steal from you, but he or she can't steal "you" in the natural. However, it's another story in the spiritual realm, which we will discuss later.

It's Not Just Natural

Now that we know what the loosely used term, "identity," means, it's important to know that identity theft is not limited to just our "natural" identities. When we hear the term, "identity theft," we logically assume that the threat is to our natural identities. By implication, our natural identities would be inherently present or established when we are born. However, as you've seen, our identities have also become tied to other things, such as our good name, credit and finances. If an identity thief steals your natural identity, it would not change the essence of who you are. In fact, the impersonator would not actually steal your "identity," but rather some superficial information about you. Moreover, your "real" identity goes much deeper than your identification numbers and financial resources.

Just as we have a natural identity, we also have a "spiritual" identity. We need to explore what is meant by "spiritual identity," which refers to our "real" identity that comes from God. Unlike our natural identity that can fluctuate based on our or others' conduct, our spiritual identity is permanent and secure based on our relationship with God. Well, there's not only identity theft in the natural realm, there's also identity theft in the spiritual realm too. Satan desires to take advantage of us by "stealing" our spiritual identities and destroying our relationships with God.

So far, most of the discussion about identity theft has focused on the natural crime, which sets the foundation for the spiritual one. In order for us to fully comprehend the identity theft that's taking place in the spiritual realm, we have to examine what's been happening in the natural. As previously stated, we know that God's order is first natural, and then spiritual.

> "Howbeit that was not first which is spiritual, but that which is natural; and afterward that which is spiritual."
>
> 1 Corinthians 15:46

This scripture points out that the "spiritual" did not come first, but rather the "natural." Here, the apostle Paul is speaking of the creation of the natural man, Adam, who came first, and then the spiritual man, Jesus Christ, who came last. In God's order of creation, the spiritual follows the natural. For example, if you want to witness to an unbeliever who is homeless and hungry, you have to address his or her natural needs (clothing and food) before you can deal with the spiritual need (salvation). With this insight, I was able to understand the connection between the theft of my natural identity and my spiritual identity.

Since the natural perspective is essential to our spiritual understanding, we will analyze the natural crime of identity theft first. I will get into more specifics about my personal story, so that you have a clear picture of how this crime happens in the natural.

I had finally made up my mind to refinance my house, so I called the mortgage company one day to finalize the details. They had already prepared the paperwork, so the only thing left was to get a copy of my credit report. I thought this was a minor detail since there had not been any changes in my credit history. To my surprise, I was advised to check my credit report because there was something "strange" going on. I was caught totally off guard and couldn't believe what I was hearing. I immediately requested copies of my credit reports from all three credit reporting agencies. When I discovered all the new credit card accounts and the mortgage loan that had been fraudulently opened up in my name, I thought it was going to take me out. Mentally, I felt as if I had been beaten, robbed and violated in the most inhumane way. I was overwhelmed and emotionally distraught, but all I could think about was how it would affect me financially. I kept asking myself, "How could anyone have gotten access to my information?" Even as an attorney, I didn't have a clue about what I needed to do to resolve this mess.

Like most of you, I had heard about identity theft, but I didn't realize what it meant until I experienced it first-hand. While I was riding down Interstate 75N in Detroit a while back, I noticed a sign, "Identity: A lifetime to build, a second to lose," which got my attention. I had spent years building my credit, and a slick thief stole it in a matter of seconds. It was one of the most humiliating and embarrassing times of my life. When some of my creditors saw the significant change in my credit history before I was aware of it, they began to lower my credit card limits or close my accounts without the courtesy of a phone call or letter asking for an explanation. I had always paid my credit card bills on time, but these companies were only concerned about protecting their own interest (not mine). Once I was able to recuperate from this awful roller coaster ride, I began dealing with the aftermath of the identity theft. I was determined to put the pieces of my life back together. The identity thief was living the life that I should have been living, and it was up to me to fight to get my stolen identity back.

At this point, I was still pondering why we are so willing to fight for natural things, which are stolen from us. Yet, we usually don't have the same passion when it comes to spiritual things. When I was in elementary school, a bully came up to me and punched me in my head because he wanted my lunch money. I instinctively started fighting him back without even thinking about it. Similarly, most of us will fight for natural things, including our jobs, homes or cars, if there is a threat of them being taken from us. On the contrary, we don't tend to fight as hard, if at all, for our spiritual treasures, such as our faith, peace or joy, because we obviously don't value them as much. If we lose our faith, we assume that our fate is sealed and tend not to take any action.

On the other hand, when my natural identity was stolen, I was persistent about getting it back. I felt like my good name and integrity were on the line, and I had to do something about it. Based on my reaction to the theft, I realized that my identity was too closely tied to my creditworthiness, so I had to make some changes in my life. However, when I knew that my spiritual identity had also been compromised, I found myself sitting back and waiting for someone else to act on my behalf to get it back. Have you ever experienced this type of struggle with your spiritual identity? Regardless of your answer, you can rest assured that it's just a matter of time before the enemy tries to hijack your identity.

Spiritual I-Jacking

Similar to our natural identity being hijacked by an identity thief, our spiritual identity can be what I call "I-jacked." As you know, criminals will stop at nothing to get our natural identities, so they can steal whatever we have of value. The same holds true in the spiritual realm as well. Just like natural identity theft can cause great financial loss, spiritual identity theft usually results in significant, spiritual loss. In addition, the spiritual crime ultimately strips us of our God-given identities. That's why the enemy of our soul, Satan, is trying to steal our spiritual identity every day. The challenge is to figure out how to win this battle against him for our identities.

Do you know if you are a victim of spiritual identity theft? It happens when someone tries to steal who you are in Christ. It typically occurs when you don't know who you are, and it is designed to stop you from accomplishing what you were put on this earth to do. God created each of us for a unique purpose and put in us every gift and talent that we need to fulfill our purpose. The enemy knows that once you understand who you are, you will be "purpose driven" and no one can stop you. If you don't even know it's happening, Satan will literally take you to the cleaners. Sometimes, your spiritual identity is stolen one piece at a time. Even if the enemy doesn't actually "steal" your identity, just giving him access to it is enough for him to do some major damage. For this reason, Satan looks for every opportunity to snatch your spiritual identity and make a clean break.

Most of us have already been a victim of spiritual identity theft, but we may not know it even if we know that something is missing in our lives. My real identity had been stolen many years ago, but I only fully recognized it about ten years ago. However, I can't pinpoint the exact day or time when it happened or how it happened, but who's going to notice this kind of identity theft anyway?

When our spiritual identities are stolen from us, we usually don't panic because we don't even know that our identities are missing or exactly what we're missing. Don't worry because we will inventory our actual loss in Step 2 of the recovery process, so we know exactly what we're looking for.

While my life was turned upside down when my natural identity was stolen, it was minor when compared to the attack against my spiritual identity. While I was going through my crisis, I had a very troubling dream that left me pondering what was going on in my life. In the dream, I was standing outside watching a man speaking from a platform, which was near a big house. There were hundreds of people listening attentively to his every word, but I knew that he was an "imposter" of some kind. The man knew that I could see that he was a fake, but he kept talking to the crowd. All of a sudden, I was inside the house lying in a bed and could not move although I was not physically tied down. I was very frustrated because I was being held against my will and knew that the man was up to no good. I heard a soft voice coming from somewhere, but I could not figure out what was being said. Then, I realized that it was the Holy Spirit reminding me of the Word of God, and I heard scriptures such as, "I can do all things through Christ that strengthens me...I am more than a conqueror." At that point, I was able to get out of the bed and was eager to run out the door. However, when I got up, the man disappeared and would not show his face. I knew then that I was missing something and could not leave without it. My friend was there with me, and she was trying to urge me to get out while I still could. I realized that the man had stolen my purse, which I later found out represented my "identity." I kept emphatically saying, "I am not leaving without my purse!" Finally, the actual wallet that I had at that time fell out of thin air, but I kept demanding my purse from the man. He was still hiding and would not show his face, but eventually he returned my actual purse. When I woke up, I knew the dream had a profound meaning, but I didn't have the full revelation yet.

I prayed about the dream and asked the Lord to reveal to me what it meant. I was blown away by what I learned. The man in the dream represented Satan, who had duped all of the people who were willing to listen to him. Although I knew he was a fraud, I opened the door for him because I was uncertain about my identity, maybe out of doubt or fear. That's the reason that I ended up in the house because I had unknowingly given him control over me. However, once I heard the Word and knew who I was, I was free to leave. In effect, I had allowed Satan to seize my identity (the purse which held my wallet and identification) without my knowledge, but I refused to leave without it. However, he had conceded that I had been released from bondage, but he didn't want me to "fully" know who I am in Christ and was still trying to hold on to pieces of my identity. Once I discovered that my identity was missing, the man hid and would not face me.

> "Submit yourselves therefore to God. Resist the devil, and he will flee from you."
> *James 4:7*

After I submitted to God and resisted the enemy, he had to flee. When I demanded the return of my purse, he was willing to give me the wallet, which represented only a piece of my identity. Remember that I was trying to put the "pieces" of my life together. However, when he knew that I was not backing down, he also reluctantly returned my purse. At that point, I had my "entire" identity back, and I walked out the door completely free.

The Lord gave me this dream in response to my prayers about wanting to be made "whole." I knew that something was missing in my life, but I didn't know exactly what it was. When I initially had the dream, I didn't realize that it was my spiritual (not natural) identity that Satan was really after. The enemy wanted to steal my spiritual identity, so that I would not have a clue about who I am, forcing me to forfeit my spiritual treasures.

In the same manner that the theft of your natural identity disconnects you from your financial resources, spiritual identity theft essentially disconnects you from your spiritual resources...prayer, fasting, devotion, and the Word of God. However, there's one important difference between the two crimes – how the stolen items are used.

With natural identity theft, the thieves steal your identity to use it to their advantage. With spiritual identity theft, nobody cares about your identity. Once your spiritual identity is stolen, it is thrown away like old trash. Spiritual identity theft usually causes its victims to sit and do nothing about it. Since you don't even know what you're missing, it's so easy to cover up the underlying void by pursuing other things. If the painful awareness ever does surface, it gets pushed down as soon as possible with various distractions to keep you from thinking about it. It appears as if natural identity theft is much more important than spiritual identity theft, but more is at risk in the latter crime. Just like natural identity theft, it can be a long and difficult process to reclaim one's spiritual identity if it's ever stolen.

Whether you realize it or not, spiritual identity theft has been going on for a long time. There were different tricks of the trade long ago, but the results were the same. Remember when Jacob stole the identity of his older brother, Esau, in exchange for a bowl of stew in the book of *Genesis*. As the oldest, Esau was entitled to the birthright and the blessing from his father, Isaac. Since Esau apparently didn't understand the value of his birthright, he voluntarily gave it away to Jacob to satisfy his hunger. Once Esau realized that he had given away his "identity," he was furious. However, it was too late for him to do anything about it. There was no cancelling the deal with his birthright and getting a new one. To make matters worse, Jacob deceived his father and also stole Esau's blessings with the help of his mother. When Esau finally knew what Jacob had done and what all he had lost, he was devastated. Not only had he lost his natural inheritance, his spiritual identity had been stolen from him at the same time. Just one bad decision by Esau led to a chain of events that changed his life forever.

Did you even know that Satan had tried to steal your identity, leaving you with a mammoth, spiritual debt that you couldn't repay? Satan seeks to steal your identity in Christ and spiritually bankrupt you. He doesn't want you to know how closely connected you are to Christ. This predator wants to make you feel distant from Him when you're actually close, guilty when you are actually forgiven and alone when nothing can separate you from His love. Satan wants you to forget who you are, whose you are, and the spiritual resources that are available to you through your relationship with Christ. You may know that the enemy is after your spiritual identity, but do you really know and understand the risks?

Chapter 3

What's Really At Risk?

Now that we know that identity theft is at an all time high, we have to understand the potential risks associated with it. Our identity is clearly at risk of being stolen, so we need to know what's really at risk. When we hear the word "risk," identity theft is usually not the first thing that comes to mind. We typically think of things, such as credit risks, market risks, health risks, insurance risks or investment risks. What's interesting is that all of these types of risks have one thing in common – potential financial exposure. In light of the tough economy, these are the types of risks that are on most people's minds. We wonder about the decrease in the value of our 401K or the company stocks that we've invested in; the increased cost of our health insurance; and the limited credit and loans available to pay off our debts. The reason we are so concerned about these risks is because we fear the financial impact. If we get hit hard in our pocketbooks, of course it gets our attention. As a result, we tend to take action faster to manage or minimize the risks as much as possible once we know what we're exposed to.

The Last To Know

The real problem with the crime of natural identity theft is the victim's lack of knowledge. The FTC has stated that the average victim is unaware of the problem for twelve months. Identity theft can happen to you without you doing anything to expose yourself or even knowing about it. How can you guard against a risk if you're not even aware that it exists? On a recent ABC news report on the risks of identity theft, the reporter said, "It's no longer a matter of *whether* we will be a victim of identity theft, but a matter of *when*." Despite this reality, most people don't even realize their identity is at risk of being stolen until it's too late. Let me ask you a few questions to help you identify your own potential risk of identity theft: 1) Do you give your credit card to the waiter to pay for dinner at restaurants? 2) Do you withdraw money from an ATM? 3) Do you give out your personal information to make purchases online? 4) Do you keep your social security card in your wallet? or 5) Do you throw pre-approved credit card offers in the trash? If you answered yes to one or more these questions, you are definitely at risk. Once you know the risks, you're held accountable if you allow it to happen. The real question is now that you know, what are you going to do about it?

It's important to know that our perception of risk determines how we judge our own exposure. It usually comes from our personal experiences or other people's stories. I read a very interesting article entitled, *What Should You Worry About,* by Steven D. Levitt and

Stephen J. Dubner (*Houston Chronicle*, October 18, 2009), which dealt with the perception of risk. The article included the statement, "Humans are good at many things...but we're quite bad at assessing risk." They pointed out that most people worry about things that are unwarranted, such as airplane crashes and lightning strikes, instead of things we should be concerned about, like heart disease and the flu. The key point was that in order to know the potential risk of anything, we need to determine what's actually dangerous. Otherwise, we will find that our fears are not in proportion to reality for certain topics.

For example, one question asked was, "Who are you more afraid of: strangers or people you know?" If you don't know the real risk, it's logical to select "strangers" as your answer. Then, they presented some shocking statistics: 3 out of 4 murder victims knew their assailants and about 7 out of 10 rape victims knew theirs. As for the crime of identity theft, they stated that most of us fear "nameless, faceless perpetrators." However, the article pointed out that nearly 50% of identity theft victims are ripped off by someone they know. And nearly 90% of those thefts happened offline, not on the internet. Unlike the old cliché, perception is not always reality. Moreover, it's important that you know the risks of whatever you're trying to protect yourself against, especially when it comes to your identity.

Being the analytical person that I am, I constantly assess all kinds of risks in my daily life. However, my identity was not even in the equation. That's one reason why I was so devastated about having no control over my identity being stolen. Since I was doing everything in my power to prevent the nightmare of identity theft, the idea of risk rarely crossed my mind. I had heard all of the horror stories about the crime, but I didn't think that it would happen to me. Then, when I found out that the identity thief was a relative, it really added insult to injury. I had been duped by someone who apparently knew enough about me to steal my identity.

Even when you know the risk and have taken steps to minimize it, you can still become a victim of identity theft. For example, I usually carry my luggage on the plane when I travel because I know the risk of it being lost or stolen if I check it. When I reluctantly checked my luggage on a trip to Miami a few years ago, I had a bad feeling about it. I went straight to the baggage claim area after I arrived at my destination, but my luggage never came out. I immediately started looking around in a panic and noticed a man with luggage like mine near the exit door. As he was about to exit the terminal, I boldly approached him and asked to see the tag on the luggage. I quickly identified it as mine and claimed it. Strangely, he apologized and said he didn't realize that it was not his, which was clearly a lie. Although I had identified the risk of checking my luggage, I had actually assumed the risk when I decided to check it anyway.

However, we can't afford to assume any risk when it comes to our identity. Some people are desperate enough to steal the names and credit of their family members and friends to keep up with their lifestyles or just to get by.

Now, I guess it's time to let the truth out of the bag -- the identity thief who stole my identity was one of my younger cousins. I was devastated to find out it was her and could not believe that she could look me in the face while she was doing her scheming. Moreover, I realized that my risk was actually greater than I could have ever imagined.

Now that we've discussed the risk involved with natural identity theft, let's apply it to the spiritual realm. When it comes to our spiritual identity, we need to also know the real risks of it being snatched by Satan. If we open the door for the enemy, he will definitely come in. The better we know our risks, the more we can protect ourselves from potential exposure. If we don't know who we are in Christ, our spiritual identities are at risk of being stolen. As believers, we already have a higher risk of being a target because Satan considers us to be a real threat. Let me clarify that we *should* be a threat to his earthly kingdom, but that depends on us. If we are faking and shaking in our walk, our risk is much lower because we just blend in with the rest of the world. I am talking about the folks who say one thing, but do another. Moreover, we underestimate the risk to our spiritual identities because we don't know what it's really worth.

For All It's Worth

In order to quantify our risk of natural identity theft, we need to determine the "value" of what we're trying to protect. The more valuable an item is, the greater risk there is of it being stolen. The value of something is relative because what's valuable to one person may be worthless to another.

I remember the time when one of my friends was proudly wearing her engagement ring, when her fiancé decided to marry someone else without bothering to tell her. She was so distraught that she kept the ring on for a few days until reality finally set in. She decided to go to a pawn shop to see how much she could get for it. The cashier offered her about $200 for the ring, which she knew was worth more. I told her that she needed to let him feel her pain, and he might offer her more money for the ring. I went back into the same pawn shop later that day and told the cashier the tragic story about the cheating fiancé. As I had hoped, he offered me twice as much for the same ring. It was amazing how he placed more value on the ring because I made it sound more valuable.

It's a sad reality that a crook can easily put a value on your "identity" as it relates to your material possessions. In turn, your identity has been reduced to what and how much you can purchase with it. It boils down to one simple question, "What is your identity worth?" The higher your credit ratings are, the more value they will have to a potential identity thief and the more risk they have of being stolen.

I worked hard to maintain my high credit score, but I never realized that it was increasing my risks of identity theft. While I placed value on my good name and creditworthiness, the crook was more interested in what she could purchase with my "good" identity. Now if my credit score had been 300 or lower, I probably would not have been as appealing to a thief.

When it comes to avoiding identity theft, we need to understand not only the value that we attach to our own identity, but also the value that a thief will place on it. Sometimes, the thief sees the value in our stuff more than we do.

Until we fully understand the value of our spiritual identity, it will be difficult for us to assess the level of our individual risks of spiritual identity theft. In 2 *Kings* 4, there is a powerful example of a widow who had to learn the "value" of what she had when things seemed hopeless in her life. In that scripture, the woman's husband had died, and she was left with a lot of debt. The creditors were coming to take her two sons to satisfy the debt, and she was in a desperate situation.

> "Now there cried a certain woman of the wives of the sons of the prophets unto Elisha, saying, Thy servant my husband is dead; and thou knowest that thy servant did fear the LORD: and the creditor is come to take unto him my two sons to be bondmen. And Elisha said unto her, What shall I do for thee? tell me, what hast thou in the house? And she said, Thine handmaid hath not any thing in the house, save a pot of oil."
>
> *2 Kings 4:1-2*

The widow went to the prophet Elisha for help, and he asked her a critical question, "What do you have in your house?" She responded that she didn't have anything, except a jar of oil. Although she didn't think the oil had any value, she at least realized that she did have "something" in her house. She went from just having a problem to seeing the potential to fix it. Her husband had left her what she needed to sustain her family, but she had to see the value in it. Elisha told her to go borrow as many pots as she could from her neighbors and fill them up in her house, and she quickly obeyed. After all was said and done, every pot was filled with oil, and there was still some left over. I call it the "faith that fills." The woman had what she needed the whole time, but she had to recognize the value of what was already in her house. Similarly, we need to understand the value of our identities. Otherwise, it will be easy to overlook them like the widow did with the "miracle" oil. When we take our identities for granted and don't realize how valuable they are, the identity thief will be ready to swoop right in and take them from us. If we know the real value of our identities, we should have a good idea of why they are at risk.

However, many people still don't think their identity is valuable for whatever reason – they don't feel worthy or they have a bad self-image. This kind of thinking allows their identity to be tampered with because they likely won't do much to protect it.

I chaired the National Bar Association Women Lawyers Division's "Respect Yourself" Mentor Program to help at-risk teenage girls learn the importance of respecting themselves and others. When the program was initially launched, I did an icebreaker to teach the girls about their "value." I showed them a crisp, new $100 bill and asked who wanted it. Every hand quickly went up with shouts of, "I want it. I want it." I began to mutilate the bill by stepping on it, crumbling it up, wetting it, getting it dirty and doing anything to destroy it. Then, I asked again who wanted the $100 bill and everyone still wanted it. I explained to them that the reason they still wanted it was because no matter what was done to the bill, it never lost its value. In turn, despite all of the negative things that had been said or done to the girls, they still retained their value.

None of those things could change the girls' true identity and who they really are. I thought it was intuitive for them to reach that conclusion. However, when I did the icebreaker for the second program, there were a couple of girls who didn't want the $100 bill after the mutilation because they said it was dirty. These girls apparently didn't understand the value of their own identity. When we don't know the value of something, it's easier for us to just toss it away. I told the girls that when they don't know the value of their minds, bodies and hearts, they are more apt to just freely give them away to the first taker. It's just like throwing precious pearls (their identity) into a pig pen and letting the swine trample all over them.

> "Give not that which is holy unto the dogs, neither cast ye your pearls before swine, lest they trample them under their feet, and turn again and rend you."
> Matthew 7:6

The only reason someone would throw something precious away is if he or she doesn't think it has value. Be careful with your "identity" because if you don't know its value, you may inadvertently throw it away and think nothing of it. It's critical that you understand the value of your spiritual identity because it will always be under attack by the enemy.

The Silent Attack

Even when you know the risks, your identity can still be attacked before you even know it. Early detection is the key to minimizing any damage that is caused by identity theft. You can be caught totally off guard if you're not expecting the attack. The more aware and up to date you are on how these thieves work, the better prepared you are to prevent their attempts and deal with them swiftly if they do attack.

Remember that the identity thief's attack is "silent," so you usually will not even see it coming until it's too late. When the thief steals your identity, the purpose of his attack is to use it up and then trash it after it no longer has value. Once you realize that your identity is at risk, you better get ready for the attacks from the predators. If they don't come, great! But if they do, you will be ready. Remember the old saying, "Hope for the best, but plan for the worst."

Now that you know what the identity thief wants, you have to stay alert to any signs of attack to stop the thief in his or her tracks. I was completely caught off guard when the identity theft happened to me.

About six months ago while I was uploading my photos to Photobucket, I experienced a silent attack on my "identity." I tried to work around a pop-up ad that kept moving around the screen, and then clicked the "X" box to close it out. I finished uploading my photos with no problem. However, later that night, my computer was flashing the words, "Your computer has been infected" with a warning to download security software. Instead, I shutdown my computer and rebooted it, not realizing that I was allowing the virus to infiltrate my program files. Though I had antivirus software, I didn't receive any alerts about the virus. Somehow the virus was able to "silently" get through when I closed the pop-up ad. When I checked my antivirus software history, the virus was listed as a low threat. I was on the computer for over four hours trying to resolve the problem myself, but I eventually had to turn it over to the experts.

What if a similar, nasty virus attacked your spiritual identity and started infecting your heart and mind? Then, malicious programs, like Trojans and spyware, could run in your mind and cause you to lose your spiritual memory. In turn, you would lose your memory of who you are without you even being aware of it. If you think you have been infected by this "spiritual identity" stealing virus, you have to be prepared to figure out what's missing from your life and take steps to avoid future attacks. This is essentially how spiritual identity theft works, where the enemy wants to attack your mind and steal your identity.

Even if your computer is safe and you've taken steps to protect your natural identity, how safe is your spiritual identity? Similar to Satan's attempted theft of Jesus' identity in the wilderness, this culprit also seeks to steal your identity. You may not even realize when your identity is under a spiritual attack. However, you may see the signs – you stop reading the Bible, praying, fasting, meditating, talking to God or going to church – but you may choose to ignore them. The enemy is glad when you respond that way because it makes his job easier. Since your spiritual identity is like the operating system of a computer, Satan is determined to attack your internal "spiritual hard drive" to get your life to crash. In addition, your spiritual immune system also resides in your spiritual identity. If he destroys that immune system, your life would be open to the enemy's future silent attacks.

No Guarantees

The purpose of assessing your risks of identity theft is so that you know where you are most vulnerable. Anytime you give out your personal information or make it accessible, you are vulnerable to attacks from an identity thief. Although you may know the risk, have assessed the risk and taken steps to minimize the risk, there is still no guarantee that you will not become a victim of identity theft. As in my case, I naively thought that I had taken the necessary steps to protect my identity, but my actions didn't stop it from actually happening. Although you are careful with your personal information, driver's license, social security number or bank or credit card numbers, and check your credit reports regularly, you could still become a victim of this terrible crime. Even in an ideal situation, you can only reduce your risk of identity theft, but not eliminate it.

According to Javelin, 50.2 million Americans were using credit monitoring services as of September 2008. I was amazed at this statistic, which tells me that people are afraid of becoming victims of identity theft and have decided to rely on outside services to protect them. There are different types of identity protection services that can monitor your information, such as credit reports, public records, credit cards and social security number. These services may do the best they can to monitor and protect your identity, but the bottom line is no product or service is absolutely foolproof.

We've all seen those "100% money back guarantees" for services that claim to protect our identities from being stolen. Like the commercial with the CEO of Lifelock, Todd Davis, who shows his social security number on a truck and dares thieves to try to steal his identity, which is exactly what they did. According to *Phoenix New Times* (May 13, 2010), Davis has had his identity stolen 13 times while using LifeLock. This identity theft protection service backs its service with a $1 million guarantee. If you become a victim of identity theft because of a failure in their service, they promise to help you fix it, up to $1 million. However, the "guarantee" is useless if you have to prove that a fault in their system resulted in your identity theft. According to a FTC news release (March 9, 2010), LifeLock, Inc. has agreed to pay $11 million to the FTC and $1 million to a group of 35 state attorneys general to settle charges that the company used false claims to promote its identity theft protection services. The news release includes the Illinois Attorney General, Lisa Madigan's statement, "This agreement effectively prevents LifeLock from misrepresenting that its services offer absolute prevention against identity theft because there is unfortunately no foolproof way to avoid ID theft." This statement reaffirms the reality that there are "no guarantees" when it comes to identity theft.

Like your natural identity, there is no guarantee that Satan will not try to steal or help you lose your spiritual identity. However, unlike the identity theft protection services, God does guarantee that He will not walk away if your identity does get stolen.

> "...for he hath said, I will never leave thee, nor forsake thee."
> *Hebrews 13:5*

He knows the risks that you are up against with the enemy, and He has promised never to leave or forsake you. In fact, He is committed to helping you to get your identity back because He is the one that gave it to you. You can't put your trust in man, but you can trust in God to protect your spiritual identity. He desires to hold your spiritual identity for safekeeping if you just allow Him to do so. Once you know that something is wrong, you need to inventory the loss and figure out exactly what's missing from your life.

STEP 1
Review Questions

1) Have you ever experienced an identity crisis? Was it natural or spiritual? What happened in your life that led to the crisis (be specific and list every event)? Were you able to identify your problem? If so, how did you resolve it?

2) Have you ever suffered from spiritual amnesia? Do you know what caused it? What steps have you taken to restore your memory of who you are (e.g., prayer, reading the Bible, fasting or talking to your pastor)?

3) Has your natural identity been stolen? What happened (e.g., someone stole your credit card or checks)? How long did it take you to discover the theft? How did you feel during the process?

4) Has your spiritual identity been stolen or lost? What happened to make you doubt or question who you are (e.g., divorce, job loss, death of a loved one, financial problems)? What impact has it had on your life? How does it compare to natural identity theft?

5) Did you know that your spiritual identity was at risk of being stolen? If so, did you think it was a low or high risk (explain why)? What steps have you taken to minimize the risk?

6) On a scale of 1 to 10 with 10 being the highest, how valuable do you think your identity is? What is the basis for the number you selected? Would your response have been different five years ago? Why or why not?

STEP 2

INVENTORY
The Actual Loss

"Either what woman having ten pieces of silver, if she **lose** one piece, doth not light a candle, and sweep the house, and seek diligently till she find it?"

Luke 15:8

POETIC EXHORTATION
The Actual Loss

My identity had already been taken,

But I didn't know until I was awakened,

I had to do an inventory of all of my loss,

Then I started counting up all the costs,

While I kept searching to find the "real" me,

And confirm the true source of my identity.

STEP 2
Overview

The second step in the process of recovering your stolen identity is to <u>inventory</u> the actual loss. After you identify what's missing, you must do a preliminary personal inventory of what you know or believe has actually been stolen from you. This step requires a self-assessment before taking any action. It's one thing to know that a burglar broke into your house and something is missing, but it's another to know exactly what was stolen. You have to know what is missing or stolen before you can even prepare your inventory.

How fast you are able to inventory your loss depends on the condition of your house. If your house is junky or out of order, it will take longer to discover what was taken. I recall when my mother told my sister to always be alert when she came in the house alone after school. One day when my sister came home, she noticed that the photos were knocked off the wall in the hallway. She took off running to a neighbor's house. In fact, someone had broken into our house and stolen our electronics. Because our house was in order, it was easy for us to figure out what had been stolen.

It's time to do spring cleaning, so we all need to get our houses in order, naturally and spiritually. Depending on what we find during our inventory, we may have to throw some items out, but hold on to others.

Before I could even contact anyone about my natural identity theft, I had to do an inventory to determine what was missing. I created a list of all the items that had been stolen before I contacted the police and federal agencies, so they could help me recover my stuff. We have to take the same approach when it comes to our spiritual identities.

REFLECTIONS ON
Identity Theft

"There's so many stolen identities in criminal hands that identity theft could easily rise 20 times."
        Thomas Harkins, COO of Edentify
Former Director of Mastercard Fraud Division
                        USA Today 2006

"If we don't act now to safeguard our privacy, we could all become victims of identity theft."
                                      Bill Nelson

Chapter 4

Don't Let Your Guards Down

Before you can start to inventory your actual loss from identity theft, you need to figure out how it happened in the first place. By now, you know that identity theft can be very frustrating, especially when a thief has stolen your identity and run up thousands of dollars in debt in your name. Many innocent victims end up dealing with the aftermath of identity theft, so it's important that you understand how to protect yourself before it happens. If we were trying to protect our cars, we would lock the doors or keep them in the garage. But how do we put a lock on our identities? Our personal identifying information is mostly in someone else's hands, so we have little or no control over what happens to it.

As discussed in Chapter 3, there is no question that your identity is at risk of being stolen by some conniving thief at any time. After your risk assessment, you should know the areas where you are most vulnerable. If you don't take security measures to protect your identity, you have, in effect, decided to assume the risk of it being stolen. Your identity, especially your credit history, can open the door for a job, car or mortgage loan, lower interest rates and other benefits, which most people take for granted. If your good name and credit are blemished, it can take years for you to clean it up. This fact alone should be enough to make you more proactive about protecting your identity. However, most people pay more attention to securing their cars than protecting their personal data. Identity thieves are a lot like car thieves and will go to desperate lengths to get what they want. If the predators really want your personal information badly enough, they will probably get it. When you don't try to protect your identity, you make the thieves' job easy.

Why do you fail to take any precautionary steps to safeguard your identity? Is it because you don't really understand the seriousness of the crime or don't think it could happen to you? If you are not concerned or worried about becoming a victim, then you definitely should be. Once you know the risks of identity theft, it's up to you to protect yourself. Your best chance of deterring identify theft is having the right protection.

Are You Protected?

We may think we're adequately protected from identity theft, but are we really? The term, "protected," implies that steps have been taken to guard against a known risk. If we want to protect our identities, we have to take measures in advance to minimize the risk of it being stolen before any harm actually occurs. It's not enough to be in a reactive mode when it comes to identity theft. We can't afford to play the "sit back and wait" game. Once our identities are stolen, it's a little too late to try to protect them.

The more we know about how our identity is stolen, the better prepared we will be to protect ourselves. In Chapter 3, you were asked several questions to help you identify your potential risk. As you know, thieves can obtain your personal information in a number of ways, from stealing mail to pretending to be a loan officer and ordering a copy of your credit report. Once an identity thief has your information, they can wreck your good name and credit. Bills are run up in your name, your credit gets trashed, and you have to argue with those bill collectors over money that you haven't even spent. Almost every aspect of your life becomes an open book, and it's a long and dreadful process to resolve everything.

Sometimes, it feels like the only way we can "protect" our identities is for us to never leave the house, don't answer the phone, don't use the computer and close all bank, credit and loan accounts. The reality is that we have to step up our game because the thieves have stepped up theirs. You have to be just as creative as the thieves are with their trickery when it comes to protecting your identity. While it's not difficult to figure out what the risks to your identity are, the issue is what you can do about it.

With the rise of identity theft, many people are concerned about keeping their personal identity protected. After I learned that my identity had been stolen, I immediately placed an initial fraud alert for 90 days on my credit file with all three credit bureaus. In order to extend the alert to seven years, I had to provide them proof of the identity fraud. With the fraud alert, all creditors are supposed to contact me on my listed phone numbers before issuing any credit in my name. I felt as if this gave me some level of protection, however, I quickly realized that the alert only works to protect me when it's enforced by the creditors.

When I applied for a new account, I told the retailer that their credit department would have to call me before the credit could be approved. On the contrary, I was able to open the account that day and didn't get a phone call until a week later. By that time, an identity thief could have maxed out the account and moved on to his or her next victim. However, once my fraud alert expired, I realized that some protection was better than none.

We can protect our natural identity by checking our credit reports, shredding bank statements, only shopping on secure websites and being careful about sharing personal information. But, how do we protect our spiritual identities? Before we can protect them, we must understand what our "spiritual identity" is. In other words, we must know who we really are spiritually. We can only learn who we are from our Creator. God has told us who we are in the Bible, which is our secure site. Similar to your natural identity, you must also be careful about whom you share your spiritual identity.

When Joseph shared his dream with his brothers, they began to mock him and worked to destroy his spiritual identity. The same thing can happen today. If you share intimate details of God's plan for your life prematurely or with the wrong people, the thief will come to steal what God has planted and will use the very people to whom you handed over the information.

If your identity is "in Christ," you can be certain that He will alert you of any threats to your spiritual identity and ensure that it will be protected.

Guard Your Valuables

Once you know the importance of having protection, you need to safeguard all of your valuables, especially your identity. There are literally thousands of ways that your identity can be stolen. In the course of a busy day, you may write a check or use your ATM card at the store, charge tickets to a ballgame, book a flight online, rent a car or apply for credit or a loan. Since these types of transactions are so common, you probably don't give them a second thought. However, an identity thief definitely does because he or she is an opportunist. Every time you use your personal information, it's an opportunity for the criminal to get access to it – whether it's the person taking your payment or someone looking over your shoulder when you put in your PIN at the ATM. It's like hitting the jackpot for them because they can steal your identity without you even knowing or getting suspicious.

When I check into a hotel on a trip, one of the first things that I look for in my room is a safe. As soon as I unpack my luggage, I will put my valuables, such as my laptop, purse and camera, in the safe. By putting a safe in the room, I think the hotel is basically saying that I better guard my own stuff. They are shifting the burden to the hotel guests, who are more familiar with which of their personal belongings need to be protected. If they leave their room without securing their stuff, they are in effect assuming the risk of it being stolen. We need to take the same precautions to ensure that our identities are safeguarded.

Protecting yourself from identity theft takes proactive efforts. You can't simply assume it's not going to happen to you and go on about your life like I did. I didn't think it could happen to me, but it did and the experience had a huge impact on my life. Anyone can be a target. Even, Ben Bernanke, chairman of the Federal Reserve, was a victim of identity theft in 2008 (*Newsweek*, August 24, 2009). According to *IdentityTheft.com*, it has even happened to several celebrities, like Oprah Winfrey, Tiger Woods, Robert De Niro and Martha Stewart. In this advanced electronics age, your information is publically available to anyone who wants to find it. Taking steps to protect it can reduce your chances of becoming a victim, but you can't ensure that your information will always be safe.

Additionally, some companies that we patronize have taken security measures to put the burden on us to verify our identities. We have to prove who we are before we can access our own stuff, but why not use the same measures for the thief? In the past few years, I have noticed a lot of major changes that my credit card companies have implemented as security measures to prevent identity theft. When I get a new credit card, I have to activate the card from my home telephone number. When I use my gas card, I have to put in my zip code at the pump to verify my identity. After my natural identity was stolen, my creditors added a special password for my accounts that I have to provide when I contact them regarding my account. When I use my credit card out of town, my credit card company will decline any suspicious charges until I call to verify that I am making them. These measures have been disruptive and inconvenient for me, but I do appreciate their willingness to do something to protect me. However, I have come to the realization that I need my "own" protection plan when it comes to my identity.

Many people spend their entire lives trying to establish a good financial and credit status, but they are totally devastated when they become victims of identity theft overnight. However, if they are aggressive about their identity theft protection, they have a better chance of guarding their stuff from being stolen. From a natural perspective, the key to safeguarding against loss is to watch out for the thief. Just like a security guard has to be watchful when he or she is on duty to protect his employer's property, you need to be watchful over your identity.

We know the steps to take to guard our natural stuff, and the same principles apply from a spiritual perspective. It's imperative that we watch out for our most valuable asset, our spiritual identity, before the enemy tries to steal it.

> "But know this, that if the goodman of the house had known in what watch the thief would come, he would have watched, and would not have suffered his house to be broken up."
>
> *Matthew 24:43*

Jesus encouraged His disciples to keep watch because they didn't know when the Lord would come. Since they didn't know God's timing, it was important that they were watchful. To illustrate this point, He used the analogy of a man who had advance notice that his house would be burglarized. If the man knows when the thief will come to break into his house, he would take precautions to protect himself and his belongings. Likewise, as believers, if we know that the master identity thief (Satan) has a plan to steal our spiritual identities, we should also take steps to protect ourselves.

We were cautioned to safeguard our financial information and important documents, such as our driver's license, social security numbers and birth certificates. Of greater importance is our spiritual identity, which is also at risk everyday from the invisible thief who is working behind the scenes. As believers, we must be as vigilant about protecting our spiritual identity as we are for our natural identity. This means that we must know who we are in Christ and actively engage in the protection of that identity on a daily basis. Satan desires to steal our spiritual identity or at least damage it for his own benefit. But we can stop it from happening by proactively protecting ourselves. Similar to how we protect our natural identity, we can protect our spiritual identity and stop Satan's damage by using the following tools:

1) Knowing God's Word (*Ephesians 6:17* – "And take the helmet of salvation, and the sword of the Spirit, which is the word of God:")
2) Knowing how to pray and fast (*Mark 9:29* – "And he said unto them, This kind can come forth by nothing, but by prayer and fasting.")
3) Knowing the enemy's devices (*2 Corinthians 2:11* - "Lest Satan should get an advantage of us: for we are not ignorant of his devices.")
4) Knowing your authority (*Luke 10:19* - "Behold, I give unto you power to tread on serpents and scorpions, and over all the power of the enemy: and nothing shall by any means hurt you.")

Sound The Alarm

While it's important to take precautions to safeguard your identity, you have to be ready to sound the alarm when there's a real threat to it. You must be prepared to take immediate action if your identity is actually stolen or has been compromised. Once you're alerted that someone has tried to steal your stuff, you have to quickly jump into action. Many of us have a panic button on our car remote, so we can sound the alarm if someone tries to carjack us or steal our purse or wallet in a parking lot. The reason we use the alarm is two-fold: 1) to alert other people who are around that we are in trouble, and 2) to surprise the thief and possibly get him or her to run away. When it comes to our identities, we also need to be ready to push the panic button to sound the alarm whenever it's warranted.

Even if you purchase an alarm system, it is only effective if you turn it on. You have to arm the system if you want to protect your valuables. Otherwise, you really don't have adequate protection. Having the ADT sign in the yard may keep some thieves away, but a lot of them will still check to see if the doors are locked and if the alarm system is actually on.

I had an interesting dream that increased my awareness about the importance of keeping my home alarm system on at all times, whether I am home or not. In the dream, I was in my bed asleep and woke up suddenly in the middle of the night. While lying in bed, I looked out the window and noticed a man standing outside of my house in the back yard. My first impulse was to look at the alarm system light to see if it was on, but it was turned off. I was afraid that the man would break in because my alarm was not armed, but for some reason I stayed in the bed. The man didn't move and continued to stand right in front of the door. The revelation that I got from the dream was that although my alarm was not armed, the man (who represented the enemy) could not come in because my back door was locked. The alarm system was only a secondary defense when I had my door locked. The man was waiting for me to open the door to give him access. This is the same tactic of Satan, which is to wait for us to give him an open door. He doesn't have the authority to come in our houses, so he patiently waits for us to let him in.

Assuming that your home alarm system is turned on and works properly, the alarm should automatically sound to warn you of any unwanted intruders. When the alarm does sound, the home security service should immediately alert you of the alarm if you don't contact them first. You've seen the Brinks commercial where the man kicks down the door when a woman and her son were home. The alarm went off and the intruder ran away. Then, the woman talked to the security representative, who told her that the police were on the way.

What happens when your power goes out? That same alarm system now becomes worthless. After Hurricane Ike hit Houston in 2008, my electricity went out at my house as it did for most people in my area. As a result, I couldn't turn my alarm system on. I went to stay at my sister's house for a few days and was very hesitant about leaving home without the alarm system working. When I finally came home, the power was still out. It was very hot in my house, so I eventually had to open the windows to get some air. I felt so exposed because not only was my alarm system off, I had my windows open. However, I said a prayer and went to sleep. About two hours later, I woke up startled by the loud sound of my alarm going off. I didn't know if someone was trying to break in, but thankfully my power had come back on and my alarm system was working again.

Similar to the anti-theft devices used to protect your natural possessions, you also need a security system to protect your spiritual assets. The Word of God is the "spiritual" security system designed to protect your spiritual identity. The checkpoint is your spirit. Your spiritual alarm system (the Holy Spirit) goes off when the thief tries to come in and attack you. It's similar to when the prophet Joel had to blow the trumpet and sound the alarm.

> "Blow ye the trumpet in Zion, and sound an alarm in my holy mountain: let all the inhabitants of the land tremble for the day of the LORD cometh, for it is nigh at hand;"
>
> *Joel 2:1*

The scripture begins with Joel sounding the alarm to warn the people of the nearness of the invader. He blew his trumpet, which was a ram's horn that was blown by a watchman to alert the people of great danger. He wanted them to be prepared because the day of the Lord was coming. Likewise, when your spiritual alarm goes off, you need to take heed. In order to have full protection of your spiritual treasures, you have to make sure your spiritual security system stays on at all times.

We know that the natural identity thief is after cold hard cash, but we need to know what Satan is after. Just like the criminals, he wants to steal things that are valuable. He is primarily out to steal your intangible jewels, like your joy, peace, confidence, integrity, freedom and credibility, when your spiritual alarm is off or not working properly. If he robs you of these valuables, he hopes to also take your entire spiritual identity. However, he doesn't stop there, but goes after your health, kids, marriage and relationships. After you implement your spiritual identity protection plan, you should continue to do a spiritual inventory to know where you are most susceptible to attack. When you least expect it, the enemy will be standing outside of your door waiting to get in. If your identity is in fact attacked or compromised, you must be prepared to sound your spiritual alarm to prevent any loss.

Loss Prevention

We have talked about ways to protect your identity when a thief is trying to steal it, so now we will consider how to address "loss prevention" if the enemy does get access. As you know, you don't have much control to prevent identity theft from happening. However, if the enemy does steal your personal information, your next line of defense is to prevent any loss. The term, "loss," means the harm or suffering caused by losing something. When we hear the word "loss," we typically think of things like weight loss, hair loss or hearing loss. However, how often do you hear anyone mention "identity theft loss?"

When I was on a business trip in Trinidad, my corporate credit card didn't work when I was trying to pay the change fee for my flight. I had to use my personal credit card, so I gave it to the airline representative. I thought it was taking longer than usual to run my credit card through, but I just continued to wait. The woman returned my card, and I went on my way until it was time to board the flight. When I got home, I had a message from my credit card company requesting that

I contact them about suspicious activity on my card. I returned the call and disputed the fraudulent charges. Apparently, someone had stolen my credit card number and started using it while I was on the plane. Although the thief got access to my credit, I prevented any loss to me by immediately notifying the company of the theft.

Simply being careful isn't enough to prevent loss from any type of identity theft. If you are serious about preventing the natural theft, you have to initially decide if you want to protect your own identity or get outside help with this effort. Since it can be very time-consuming and difficult to protect yourself, a lot of people are not interested in this option. If you do it yourself, like I did, you have to take a proactive approach to stay ahead of the thief. However, you may consider some of the identity theft prevention services (e.g., credit/identity monitoring) if you need help. If you are considering these services, make sure you do your homework. However, I monitor my own credit reports on a regular basis and take other steps to prevent and protect myself from identity theft. Since I've been through identity theft before, I have a good idea of what to expect. As a result, I have to develop my own loss prevention plan.

So far, most of the discussion in the book has been about a thief directly "stealing" your identity, naturally and spiritually. It's usually pretty clear when the crook actively goes after your identity by finding ways to access it. However, now we're going to focus on the "loss" of your identity, and the more subtle attempts to get you to hand over your identity, whether intentionally or accidentally. You may discover that your identity is lost or missing, but you don't know exactly what happened to it. In effect, all you know is that your identity is no longer in your possession. Moreover, you may have had some involvement in the loss, so you need to understand the role you might have played in order to prevent any further damage.

When you are trying to find a missing or lost "identity," it is similar to trying to find a missing person. I am not a detective, but I guess that it's easier for someone to find missing or lost property than it is to find missing people. I used to watch a TV show, *Without A Trace*, where a special FBI unit had to go on a fishing expedition to find a missing person in every episode. The lead agent, Jack Malone, headed up the team, which always had a tight 72 hour window to try to find the person who had disappeared without a trace. In order to find the person, the team created a timeline to track the activities of the missing person from the time that he or she was last seen until the person was reported as missing. There were so many scenarios that they had to go through before they eventually found the person. This is the same approach that's needed when our identities are missing.

I was recently reading the Sunday newspaper and saw a coupon at the bottom of the page with the heading, "Have You Seen Me?" It had a photo of a missing girl who was taken when she was two years old, and there was a photo age-processed to seventeen years old. Anyone who had seen the child or had information was directed to call "1-800-THE-LOST." All of us have seen similar requests to help find missing people whose photos are displayed on milk cartons, billboards or in magazines. I have even seen warnings about missing elderly people on the marquee on the freeway. When I see these types of signs, I immediately begin to wonder about the details leading to their abduction or kidnapping. Who took them? Where did they take them? Why did they take them? Despite all of these relevant questions, the bottom line is that they are missing. If one of the missing persons were your spouse, parent, child or friend, I would hope that you would do everything you could to find them. Why is it any different when you discover that your identity is lost or missing? Why aren't you willing to do whatever is necessary to find "you?" That's exactly what I had to do both naturally and spiritually when my identity was stolen. It was time for my face to come off the "missing" persons list. Don't you find it strange that we rarely see a heading with "We found these people"? The world seems to focus on those who are lost, but no attention is given to those who are found.

However, there is biblical example of a woman who rejoiced when she found her lost coin in *Luke 15*.

> "Either what woman having ten pieces of silver, if she lose one piece, doth not light a candle, and sweep the house, and seek diligently till she find it? And when she hath found it, she calleth her friends and her neighbours together, saying, Rejoice with me; for I have found the piece which I had lost."
> "
>
> *Luke 15:8-9*

Here, Jesus tells the parable of the lost coin after the Pharisees accused Him of spending time with sinners. In the parable, the woman had ten silver coins, but she lost one of them. Many people may have decided not to worry about the missing coin since they had nine coins left. They probably didn't want to waste too much time looking for it because they felt it wasn't worth it. However, this woman took out her lamp and searched her house until she found it. She was so excited about finding what she had lost that she called all of her friends and neighbors together to tell them. If we did the same thing today, our friends would think we were crazy to rejoice over finding a dime. When it comes to our lost identities, we should be rejoicing when we find them. Even if one or several pieces of your identity are missing, you should never give up on trying to find all of it. Your identity is out there, and all you have to do is put in the time required to get it back.

Do you think there's a difference between your spiritual identity being "lost" versus "stolen?" Does it really matter how it disappeared as long as you know it's missing? It doesn't matter if Satan is operating in his job as a pickpocket or as a flim flam man because either way he has stolen your stuff. Unlike a pickpocket who sneaks your identity out of your pocket, a flim flam man tricks you out of your money by offering you the chance to make more money. A flim flam man may approach an unsuspecting person with a wad of $100 bills and tell him or her about a new investment opportunity where their money can be tripled. If the victim takes the bait, the con man would ask him or her to give him $10K and say he will flip the money in a week. I am amazed at the number of people who fall for this type of scheme and willingly withdraw money out of their bank accounts to give it to the thief.

As a result, the predatory thief doesn't feel like he has done anything wrong because the people "voluntarily" gave him the money, but it's still theft any way you look at it – theft by deception. Even if we easily hand our identities over to him, don't be fooled – he has still "stolen" it even if we were tricked out of it. Would it matter if the same thief looked over your shoulder and wrote down your bank account number, and then later wiped out your entire account? This would be considered "identity theft," but your money is gone in either case. I threw this in for those of you who are wondering about the distinction between "losing" your identity and having it stolen. The same principle applies...it's gone. Esau can tell you that even when you're tricked out of your identity and voluntarily hand it over to the enemy, it doesn't hurt any less.

Since Esau willingly gave away his birthright, he usually doesn't receive much sympathy about his story. Some people think he got what he deserved, which is a classic case of blaming the victim. However, let's not forget the role that the identity thief, Jacob, played in the situation. He started jocking for position in his mother's, Rebekah, womb and had struggled with his own identity since the day he was born. If only he could have been the first born and received all of the perks. He was so close, but he was born seconds behind Esau. Jacob came out grabbing Esau's heel and had been trying to grab everything else since. Jacob had been going through a spiritual identity crisis, but he didn't have to because God already knew who he was. The problem was that he didn't know and thought he needed to make a name for himself. However, God had already told Rebekah that there were two nations struggling in her womb, and the older would serve the younger (*Genesis 25:23*). God had revealed that Jacob would be blessed, so all he needed to do was to wait.

The blessing already belonged to Jacob, but he thought he needed to steal it from his brother. He decided to take matters into his own hands, but you know how that turned out. Although God didn't applaud Jacob's methods, He had already ordained for Jacob to lead His people. Jacob had been wrestling all his life with "issues" involving his family, love, and most importantly, himself. He was searching for his spiritual identity, which he had essentially given up when he chose to become a trickster.

Similar to how Esau voluntarily forfeited his birthright, Satan is hoping that we will turn over our spiritual identities without a fight. He is the "original" master at identity theft and desires to trick us out of our identity as Jacob did to Esau. If we don't just give it up, Satan will try to help us "lose" our identity. He is always coming up with another devious way to steal it from us with little or no effort, but we need to do everything we can to hold on to our spiritual identities. The enemy desires to make us doubt who we are and whose we are, so that our futures will be uncertain like the twin brothers, Jacob and Esau.

Perhaps you have not necessarily lost your identity, but only temporarily misplaced it. When your identity is lost, you may not have any idea where to start looking for it. However, when it's only been "misplaced," you may be able to backtrack and find out where you left it. When you misplace something, it's usually not intentional. How many countless times have you misplaced your driver's license or other identification and it restricted your activities? For example, you may not be able to check-in at the airport without your identification.

Last year, I was getting ready to go on a business trip with some of my colleagues and discovered the day before our departure that I could not find my driver's license. I immediately got alarmed and started wondering if I had lost it. All I could think about was identity theft and how the thief could have my identification. After calming down, I started to backtrack my activities since I last saw my license. I remembered taking the license out of my wallet on the night before, but I could not recall what I had done with it. To start, I began to trace my steps on the day I discovered it was missing. All of a sudden, it hit me that I had made a copy of my license for my clubhouse reservation on that night. I went back to my copier, and sure enough the license was exactly where I had left it. I found it just in time for my trip. Since I lost it at home, the risk of it being stolen was relatively low. Conversely, when I was on a trip in London, my passport fell out of my bag without my knowledge. I had inadvertently misplaced it, but someone found it and returned it to me. Whether I find it or someone else finds it, the fact is it was only misplaced. As a result, all I had to do was figure out where it was and go get it.

Imagine not losing your identification or credit card, but misplacing who you are. What if you're fumbling around, and the hustle and bustle of life causes you to misplace yourself. Would you even know where to start looking to find you? Whether you know it or not, one of the most precious things that we can misplace is your identity. Who you are and what you become matters to God. Your spiritual identity is the foundation of your purpose and the key to the door of fulfillment.

Now, let's turn to the prevention of loss as it relates to your spiritual identity. If you've got protection, you can stop Satan in his tracks when he comes looking for your identity. Similar to your natural identity, you need someone (the Holy Spirit) who will continue to monitor your identity and be able to quickly warn you when there's a threat. Be careful not to lose or misplace your spiritual identity because the enemy is waiting to get his hands on it. At least make him work hard for it. You can boldly tell him that you know who you are in Christ and intend to remain who you are. Let him know that he isn't going to move you from your identity or take what belongs to you as a child of God. The devil thinks he is slick, but you are a step ahead of him when you have taken steps to protect yourself. Once you start living each day secure in Christ, you will be able to safeguard all of your spiritual valuables. However, you still need to inventory whatever Satan has already gotten his hands on, so you can take it all back.

Chapter 5

The Search To Find "You"

As you continue your journey toward your stolen identity, you must begin the search to find "you." Now that you know what can happen if you let your guards down, you can begin the initial inventory of your identity. You need to understand what the thief is after and what he was taken from you. If you've been through a spiritual identity crisis, you should already know that something is missing in your life. However, you may not be able to put your finger on it, which is a part of the problem. The purpose of Step 2 of this process is to help you figure out exactly what "it" is as you go through your spiritual identity search. Even if you don't know exactly what you're looking for, you have to start somewhere. The identity theft is the catalyst that leads you to do your search. To "search" means to examine a person or personal effects in order to find something lost or concealed. When you do a search, it implies that you are intentionally looking for something, rather than haphazardly or by coincidence. You are purposefully trying to find something specific that has been lost or hidden.

Have you ever done a Google search on yourself? What did you find out? If you want to find out about a person, all you have to do is put their name in a search engine on the internet. The first time that I did a search on my name, I was shocked by the wealth of information that came up about me. It's amazing how much you can find out by just doing a simple search. There are so many public search engines that offer your personal information for free or a small fee. If you can find it, you know an identity thief can also find it. Someone can pay $10 to find out where you live, where you work and who lives in your house. It's unbelievable what you can find by searching for a person with only a name and date of birth. When I was planning my 20th year high school reunion a few years ago, I was able to find about 50% of my classmates by doing a simple search.

When I discovered that my natural identity had been stolen, I had to do a search to confirm exactly what was taken. The first thing I had to do was contact the credit bureaus to report the fraud and order a copy of my credit reports. Based on what my mortgage company told me, I knew that something strange was going on. However, I needed to inventory my loss, so that I could inform my creditors and the appropriate law enforcement and federal agencies.

When it comes to our identities, it's easy just to make a couple of calls and then say we're done. If we don't figure out quickly that our identities have been tampered with, we move on to the next issue. However, we have to do a thorough search until we find out what we need to know. Knowing exactly what we have lost is essential to recovering everything.

One of the times that I misplaced my cell phone, I got a new revelation on what it means to really "search" for something. Searching may not be a quick or easy process, but it is a necessary step. While I was at the carwash one day, I received a call on my cell phone as I got out of my car. I was cleaning out my car, so I told my friend that I would call her back. I stuffed some trash in a bag and threw it into the trash can. I went inside to pay for the carwash and watched my car go through the wash cycle. I drove off in my clean car and was on my way to run my errands. I had been so busy that day that I didn't realize that I had lost my cell phone until I needed to make a call. I became frantic and started to backtrack to all the places I had been. However, I could not find my phone anywhere.

The last place where I knew for sure that I had my phone was at the carwash, so I went back there. However, the carwash was closed, but I decided to look around the outside area. As I was about to drive off, I decided to look in the trash can where I had put my trash. It was completely empty, so I was about to give up on my search. All of a sudden, I noticed a huge dumpster in the back of the carwash. As soon as I saw it, I had a strange feeling that my cell phone was in there. I used my blackberry to call my cell phone, and I thought I heard a faint ring coming from the dumpster. When I looked up at the dumpster and saw how tall and dirty it was, I decided to go home and change into an old warm-up suit and tennis shoes. By the time I got back to the carwash, it was dark outside. I had to ask myself how bad I wanted to find my phone. Before I could think about it, I was climbing up the nasty dumpster full of trash and jumped in with my gloves on. I kept calling myself until the ringing got louder. I had to dig deep until I found the trash bag with my phone in it. I could not believe that I had accidentally thrown my phone away, and I had to literally go "dumpster diving" to find it. Everyone that I told could not believe my story. However, I was determined to find my phone at any cost.

This is the same approach that some of us take with our spiritual identities. We get distracted by the cares of this life, and either throw our identities away or allow them to be stolen by a cunning identity thief. We are so busy going through our regular routine that we may not even know where to start looking for our identities once we discover they are missing. Just like I had to do, we must backtrack and go through our "past" to confirm where we left them.

Did you lose your spiritual identity at home when your spouse walked away, at work when you got fired or laid off, at church when you were overlooked for a position or at the doctor's office when you received a bad diagnosis? Once you know where you left or lost your identity, you have to be ready to do a little dumpster diving to get it back. It may not be pretty to jump into the garbage from your past, but you have to put on your gear and just jump in. As long as your search turns up your "real" identity, the rest doesn't matter. Can you hear your spiritual identity phone ringing, whether it's faint or loud? You can't be afraid to get dirty to find "your stuff." It's time for you to answer your spiritual phone. In order to find your spiritual identity, you have to be willing to search for it anywhere and at anytime.

Who Do You Think You Are?

As you begin to inventory your spiritual identity, your determination must be based on who you think you are, not what your parents, your spouse, your children, your siblings, your friends or your enemies think. This is a personal assessment, which only you should be able to do. If you know what furniture is in your house, how can someone who doesn't live with you provide the police an inventory of what was stolen from your house? Only you and God know if something is missing from your spiritual house and what it is. So, who do you think you are? Whatever you think in your heart is who you are.

"For as he thinketh in his heart, so is he:"
Proverbs 23:7

Keep in mind that who you think you are may not be who you actually are, which is why it's important to do your search.

There's an old expression, "Just who do you think you are?" It's intended to be a question that you are expected to answer based on your own perception. It requires you to do some soul searching to determine your true identity. There is a TV show, *Who Do You Think You Are?*, which deals with this very issue. It's a very interesting show that allows the viewers to take an up-close look inside the family history of various well-known celebrities, such as Lisa Kudrow, Sarah Jessica Parker, and Emmitt Smith. The program leads these celebrities on a journey of self-discovery as they examine their family trees, which reveal surprising stories that are often linked to crucial events in American history. Likewise, when you do your personal search, I think you will find some interesting facts about your past and how it has influenced who you are today. It's important to know where you've come from to help you fully understand where you are going, but it doesn't have to define who you are now.

When my natural identity was stolen, I had to do my own personal search. I knew my name and personal information, but I was still unsure about who I was after the crime took place. My good name and credit were out the window, so I was so uncertain about who I was, who I owed and how much I owed. My "identity" had been reduced down to my financial status. The need to search your identity is tied back to the identity crisis that was discussed in Chapter 1. Once you understand your crisis, you can finally do something about overcoming it.

Because of our spiritual identity crisis, we are faced with an unfortunate dilemma that we must deal with now or later. The conflict arises when we fail to recognize or acknowledge who we really are. We can never conquer issues that we are not willing to confront. We must address this issue of our identities head on and be secure in who we are in Christ. When we confront our spiritual identity crisis, we must reconcile our real identity by dealing with: 1) Who we say we are, 2) Who others say we are and 3) Who God says we are. Since this process involves a personal inventory, the focus will be on you individually.

1) **Who Do You Say You Are?**

This is a simple question that people have struggled with since the creation of time. When asked this question, most people would give their names, ages, addresses, careers or jobs and their favorite roles (e.g., husband, wife, mother, father, son, daughter or grandparent). However, is this really who they "are" as opposed to what they "do" in their various roles? If your response to this critical question depends on what you do, who you know or what you have, your spiritual identity has already been stolen.

After various points in your life, you may have had to answer the question, "Who are you?" Whether it was for a job interview, school admission or a board position, the interviewer may have asked you this broad question to solicit an array of answers. My guess is that you would tell a little about yourself and what you do..."I'm a writer, lawyer, engineer, doctor or teacher." But that's not really *who* you are – it's what you *do*. Which leads to the next question, "If what you do is who you are, who will you be when you stop doing what you're doing?" However, most people usually acquire their identities through reflecting on what they do and the people and things they identify with. For example, if someone asked you, "Who are you?" and you replied, "I am a doctor." You may identify yourself with your job and think of yourself more as a doctor rather than just a person or child of God. In turn, your identity will be based on what you "do" rather than "who" you really are.

The more we make our spiritual identity "externally" dependant on our jobs, finances, successes, families or any external object, the more we will be likely to lose this identity when we lose the external object. On the other hand, the more we make our identities "internally" dependent, the less likely we will suffer from an identity crisis where we're unsure about who we are. When people introduce me, they usually give my name and say, "She's an attorney," or "She's an author." However, that's not who I am, but simply what I do. If you ask me "Who do I say I am?" I would say, "I am a woman of God who loves the Word and walks in integrity." However, when people ask that question, they usually want to know what I "do" instead. When people ask me what I do, I say that I work at ExxonMobil. Then, they ask what I do there, and I reply that I work in the Law Department. I intentionally don't tell them what I do – an attorney. I don't think it should matter what I do if they want to get to know the "real me." Why does no one seem to really be interested in who I am or who you really are? The world wants to know about your credentials, but God is more concerned with your credibility.

Sometimes who we think we are, is not actually who we really are. For various reasons, such as sin or disobedience, we may lose sight of our real identities. For example, remember when the prophet Nathan had to confront King David about his stolen identity. God called David "a man after his own heart" (*1 Samuel 13:14*), but David could not see who he had turned into – an adulterer, murderer, etc. David was a man of war, but found himself at home when his men were at war. The first problem was that he was not in the place he should have been, so he got himself into trouble. He committed adultery with Bathsheba, and then had her husband, Uriah, killed to hide his sin. However, after he fell into sin, the Lord sent Nathan to remind David of who he really was in God's eyes. Nathan told David about a man who had done the same things that he had done. David was furious and said that "man" should be killed, but he had no idea that he was pronouncing his own demise. After David acknowledged that the man (him) was in the wrong, Nathan told him "thou art the man."

> "And Nathan said to David, Thou art the man. Thus saith the LORD God of Israel, I anointed thee king over Israel, and I delivered thee out of the hand of Saul;"
>
> *2 Samuel 12:7*

David could not see who he had turned into or that his true identity had been stolen or at least temporarily lost. Some of us go through the same thing when we are struggling with our spiritual identities even if we don't realize it. However, David was willing to acknowledge his sin and assume his God-given identity, and we need to do the same.

2) **Who Does Man Say You Are?**

Once you confirm "who you say you are," you have to examine who others say you are. How do people identify you? Do they say, "Hey, there's the man who teaches at the high school," or "That woman is president of the business group." We all have titles that others use to identify us. Jesus asked His disciples, "Whom do men say that I...am?" (Mark 8:27). Some said He was John the Baptist, Elijah or another prophet. Jesus already knew what the people were saying about Him, but He wanted to see if it had any influence on what His disciples said about Him. Jesus then asked them, "But whom say ye that I am?" Simon Peter answered and said He is "the Christ" (Mark 8:29).

What are you called by those who know you best? Do they say, "You can tell she is a Christian?" or "He is a man of God." If your identity is tied to God, it should be easy for your family, friends and coworkers to recognize it without you saying a word. What they say about you may depend on how you talk to people, treat them or act. How you live, rather than what people or you say, should testify of who you really are. Those closest to Jesus knew He was the Savior. Although His haters didn't know who He was, those closest to Him did. Do those closest to you know who you really are? I was surprised by the number of people who didn't really know me, but thought they did. We can't let the world dictate who we are because that's already been decided by God.

During my spiritual identity crisis, I tried my best to fit into the crowd in college. Rather than being the unique person that I am, I was more concerned with what people had to say about me. I was struggling with my identity and wanted affirmation from people. When my roommates went to a party that I skipped, someone told one of them that something must be wrong with me. The person couldn't understand why I didn't drink, smoke or party like some of my peers. Her comments really bothered me because I was being ostracized for doing what I went to college for – to study. Since I was focused on my education, I graduated with honors while some of my haters didn't graduate at all. I was glad that I knew what people were saying about me, but I refused to let it stop me from reaching my goals or fulfilling my purpose.

You should know by now that man's perception of you is usually far different from God's perception of you. A good example is the story about David, the eighth son of Jesse, being anointed king of Israel (1 Samuel 16:1-13). After God rejected Saul as Israel's king, He sent the prophet Samuel to Bethlehem to anoint the new king. God told Samuel to invite Jesse because one of his son's had been chosen as the next king, but He didn't tell him which one. Samuel invited Jesse to the feast, and seven of his eight sons attended. His youngest son, David, was keeping his father's sheep at that time. When Jesse's oldest son stepped up, Samuel assumed that he was the chosen one because he was tall and handsome. However, God told him that he was not the one and that His choice could not be judged by his appearance.

> "...for the LORD seeth not as man seeth; for man looketh on the outward appearance, but the Lord looketh on the heart."
>
> 1 Samuel 16:7

Jesse then brought his other six sons to Samuel, and one by one they passed before the prophet. Samuel shook his head and said that none of them had been chosen. He asked Jesse if he had another son, and he replied that his son, David, was just a shepherd boy. David's own father didn't think he was "king" material, so he didn't even invite him to the feast. Of course, David could not be the one God had chosen, but he actually was. However, David's father didn't even know who he really was or how God viewed him. In fact, Samuel anointed David as the new king of Israel. His father was basically saying that David was not qualified to be a king, but this is the same man who slew Goliath, wrote most of the book of Psalms and served as the second king of Israel. No matter what man says about you, you have to know what God says about you. What He says about you is what you should be saying about yourself.

3) **Who Does God Say You Are?**

If you want to overcome your spiritual identity crisis, you can't worry about who man says you are or even who you say you are, but stand on who God says you are. The only way you can get an accurate picture of who you really are is from God, the One who created you and knows you better than anyone else. It doesn't matter what other people say because God has already spoken. Once God says who you are, it is already settled.

> "So shall my word be that goeth forth out of my mouth: it shall not return unto me void, but it shall accomplish that which I please, and it shall prosper whereto I sent it."
>
> *Isaiah 55:11*

God's "word" cannot return to Him empty, but it has to accomplish whatever He sends it out to do. His Word has creative power and never fails to achieve its intended purpose. It's impossible for God to speak something about you, and His words come back with an "incomplete" report. When He speaks the words, they immediately go out to perform the task that He intended. Do you even know what God says about you in the Bible? Here are just a few things that God has spoken about your spiritual identity.

1) You are a child of God. *(John 1:12)*
2) You are a friend of Jesus. *(John 15:15)*
3) You are a joint-heir with Christ. *(Romans 8:17)*
4) You are more than a conqueror. *(Romans 8:37)*
5) You are accepted. *(Romans 15:7)*
6) You are a new creature. *(2 Corinthians 5:17)*
7) You are chosen. *(Ephesians 1:4)*

Although God is very clear about what He says about your identity, you may not believe it and continue to struggle with who you are. There is only one person who knows you completely, and that is God. He knows you better than you know yourself. He even knows every strand of hair on your head *(Luke 12:7)*. Like Jeremiah, God knew you in your mother's womb and had already spoken your destiny. Once you know who you really are, you are free to be who God intended you to be. However, sometimes you may hide from yourself, mainly because you don't like who you think you are. Actually, you're saying, "God you didn't do a good job, and I don't like who you made me to be." If you need a reminder of who you are, you have to continue to study the Bible. As you grow and are nourished by the Word of God, you will discover your true purpose and God's plan for your life, both naturally and spiritually. When you don't appreciate the value of your spiritual identity, you are left not knowing who you are and end up searching endlessly to find yourself.

Once you start going down this path, a spiritual identity crisis is inevitable because what you believe is in conflict with what God said about you. This conflict could be caused by your listening to or believing what others are wrongly saying about you, or it could be self-induced. We often go through life acting like someone different from who God made us to be. Most of us have had to pretend that we're someone else in a play or a skit, which was intentional. There are also many other times in our lives when we don't intend to act like we are someone different from ourselves, but we do so unknowingly. However, sometimes we know exactly what we are doing and are aware that we're putting on an act to impress somebody. People take on the role of others for many reasons, but one of them is because they don't want to be who they are.

Have you ever intentionally pretended to be someone that you were not? Like someone who was much smarter, richer or popular than you. Think about the details of that situation and why you felt the need to put on an act. What made you want people to see you differently than who you are? Only you can give the honest answer because you're in the middle of the search to find you.

We must know that our spiritual identities are based on who God says we are, and nothing else really matters. That alone dictates our eternal destinies and whether we live life to the fullest. As believers, our identities include who we are as a total package. Yes, our flaws, weaknesses, failures, fears and all. Like the old saints used to say, "God is not through me yet. I may not be who I am supposed to be, but I'm definitely not who I used to be." When I was struggling with my identity, I had to realize that God created me to be who I am. He made me exactly the way He wanted me to be from the inside out. He has always seen the best in me even when others or I wanted to see the worst in me. I am reminded of this great song, *Best in Me*, by Marvin Sapp. It reaffirms that we are better at our worst than some people are at their best. The song states that God saw the best in us when everyone else could only see the worst in us. It also says that we're His and He is ours, so it doesn't matter what we've done. God only sees us for who we are. The sooner we get that revelation; we can walk in our "real" identity. We must never forget who we are and to whom we belong.

Need A Reality Check?

Once you've searched your identity, you need to do a reality check to confirm that what you find is in line with who God created you to be. A "reality check" is an assessment to determine if your expectations conform to reality. In other words, it's an opportunity for you to consider a situation realistically. Some of us need a reality check because we may be living in a fantasy land and have been lying to ourselves about who we are. Sometimes, we think we're seeing our lives clearly, but in reality things may actually be more blurry than we realize. I had 20/20 vision until I went to law school. Before I graduated, I noticed that I couldn't see the chalkboard very well when I was sitting in the back of the room. I could read most of the words, but they were blurry so I had to strain to see them. When I finally had an eye exam, I was told that I needed eyeglasses. When I put on my first pair, it was like the whole world just lit up. I could suddenly see little things, like the birds on the light poles and the leaves on the trees, which I had no clue that I had been missing. I thought I had been seeing things clearly, but in fact my eyes had been playing tricks on me. When my vision was blurred, I could only see what was right in front of me. How could I focus on something that I couldn't even see? When you are searching for your identity, you may also not be seeing things very clearly. When that happens, you may need a reality check to determine what's real and what's not.

Do you need a reality check when it comes to your spiritual identity? Can you honestly say that you see yourself the same way that God does? Now that you know who God says you are, is that who you see when you look in the mirror? You have to make an honest assessment of yourself. You may say that you know who you really are, but you may still be struggling with issues, such as low self-esteem, inferiority and insecurity. It stems from the spiritual identity crisis that we talked about in Chapter 1 and causes your spiritual vision to be impaired. As a result, you may begin to doubt who you are and whose you are.

Let's take a closer look at your identity, so you can see it for what it really is. When you are going through your identity search, you may discover that your self-esteem has taken a big hit. We hear a lot of talk about our self-esteem, but usually the focus is on those who don't have enough. If we don't feel good about ourselves, we could suffer from low self-esteem. However, sometimes people can have too much self-esteem when they are in love with themselves. Both of these extremes are counter to what God wants for us. In scripture, we are reminded not to think more highly of ourselves than we should.

> "For I say…to every man that is among you, not to think of himself more highly than he ought to think; but to think soberly, according as God hath dealt to every man the measure of faith."
> *Romans 12:3*

Here, the apostle Paul tells us to avoid thinking too highly of ourselves, but he didn't tell us to think "low" of ourselves, either. However, he was emphasizing that we need to be realistic about who we are. It's important that we avoid the two extremes: low self-esteem and high self-esteem. However, some people still think very lowly of themselves. This is the reason that they allow others to step all over them or take advantage of them. They may feel worthless because that's what others have told them or that's what they think based on their own track record. On the other extreme, there are people who think they are the best thing since sliced bread. Those people with overly, high self-esteem have learned how to pat themselves on the back to make others take notice of them. Before they know it, they are walking around showing off their "self-made" identity. If you tell them that they are not God's gift to the world, you will probably have to lock them up. They would not believe you anyway because they are full of pride and arrogance. I called this the under vs. over inflated ego syndrome.

In the middle of the two extremes, there is another group of people who do know who they are, but intentionally try to "dumb down" so people will like them or to get affirmation. They call it "humility," but that is not true if they have to pretend to be someone they're not. I used to have a false humility when people complimented me because I was always taught not to toot my own horn. I never wanted people to think I was bragging on myself, so I felt that I needed to downplay my achievements. I was like an eagle walking around with penguins trying to make them feel better about themselves. However, the reality is that penguins will never be able to fly, so I needed to spread my wings and be who I am. However, I had somehow confused being proud of myself with being prideful. If someone asked me if I am an author, and I replied, "Not really." That's not being humble, but untruthful. If we are realistic and honest about who we are, it is more difficult for us to be full of pride.

> "Pride goeth before destruction, and an haughty spirit before a fall."
> *Proverbs 16:18*

If we do walk in pride, it will eventually lead us to spiritual destruction. However, there is a difference between being confident and being conceited. We should not cast away our "confidence" in who we are in Christ.

> "Cast not away therefore your confidence, which hath great recompence of reward."
> *Hebrews 10:35*

As believers, we should hold on to our confidence because we will be rewarded for our faithfulness. However, we must refuse to fall into the trap of conceit. If we can be honest with ourselves, a reality check will help us to see clearly who we are. If your vision is still blurry, you probably need to do another check.

On the high self-esteem end of the spectrum, the Church of Laodicea was a little overly confident and thought it was better off than it really was. Jesus sent a letter to the church through the apostle John to give them a much needed reality check. Jesus referred to them as "lukewarm" spiritually because they were content with their material wealth and unaware of their spiritual poverty.

> "So then because thou art lukewarm, and neither cold nor hot, I will spue thee out of my mouth. Because thou sayest, I am rich, and increased with goods, and have need of nothing; and knowest not that thou art wretched, and miserable, and poor, and blind, and naked:"
>
> *Revelation 3:16-17*

Jesus warned the Church of Laodicea against straddling the fence by being lukewarm instead of hot or cold. In effect, He was asking them, "Do you know who you really are?" He used strong words to describe the church, like "wretched, and miserable, and poor, and blind, and naked," which were opposite of their perception of who they were. Instead, they thought they were superior and rich. Although the church saw itself as naturally wealthy, Jesus had to let them know that their spiritual condition was bad. Did they need a major reality check or what? We desperately need to grasp who we really are and know what our true spiritual condition is before God. It is better to come in thinking a little less of yourself than thinking too highly. If you're not sure how to feel about yourself, be cautious to think less than more.

> "And whosoever shall exalt himself shall be abased; and he that shall humble himself shall be exalted."
>
> *Matthew 23:12*

The Search To Find "You"

If you humble yourself, you will be exalted. However, if you exalt yourself, you will be cast down. Which one would you prefer? I am taking the humble route. It's always better to be called forward than to be sent back. I've seen people arrive late at church and walk right up to the front row during the service. If there are no seats up front, they get escorted to the back. We need to be realistic about who we are because God already knows who we are, but it's to our benefit to figure it out.

After my natural identity theft, I had to do my own reality check because I was not seeing clearly at all. I began to lose myself during the recovery process. I quickly did an inventory of the material things that were stolen from me, but I had failed to even make a list of the spiritual things that had been snatched from me. I had lost my joy and peace, but I sat back and waited for someone to rescue me. So, I had to take steps to hold on to my spiritual resources and to overcome the fear that tried to grip me after the theft. I had to keep reminding myself that God has not given me the spirit of fear.

> "For God hath not given us the spirit of fear; but of power, and of love, and of a sound mind."
> 2 Timothy 1:7

When I realized what was happening, I was able to walk in the power, love and sound mind that God had already given me.

God has already revealed your spiritual identity to you, and there are three important things you must do to embrace it. First, you must start acting on the Word of God, not just hearing it. When you are searching for your spiritual identity, you have to be willing to look into your spiritual mirror, which is the Word of God. The Word gives you a reflection of who you are supposed to be, so you have to heed what it reveals to you. You can't just hear the Word and not act on it.

> "But be ye doers of the word, and not hearers only, deceiving your own selves. For if any be a hearer of the word, and not a doer, he is like unto a man beholding his natural face in a glass: For he beholdeth himself, and goeth his way, and straightway forgetteth what manner of man he was."
>
> *James 1:22-24*

In addition to hearing the Word, you have to do what it says. However, you may try to fool yourself into thinking that you are hearing the Word, while it's actually going into one ear and out the other. You may be able to fool yourself or others, but you can never fool God. You can no longer just talk the talk, but have to walk the walk. If you hear the Word but fail to act on it, you are like a man who glances in the mirror and forgets what he looks like when he walks away. Just minutes later, he doesn't have any idea who he is.

Have you ever looked into your spiritual mirror and forgotten what you've seen? Unfortunately, you may often hear the Word, but chose never to act on it. When you do this, it's the same as looking in a mirror and not remembering who you are. If God has already established your spiritual identity, why don't you reflect who He is? If you are truly grounded in the Word, then you will be rooted in your true spiritual identity.

Second, you must remove any hindrances to your relationship with God from your life. After my natural identity was stolen, I had to take an inventory of my own life and how the whole situation affected me. It forced me to take a deeper look at my life, which I began to see from a different perspective. While it's normal to be upset when someone steals something from you, I was like a deer caught in headlights. I was so overwhelmed that I couldn't even sleep. I needed a reality check about where I was at that point in my life. I prayed that God would reveal to me the changes that I needed to make to stay connected to the identity that He had given me. I had lost my focus by becoming consumed with trying to get payback for what happened to me. It was time for me to draw closer to God and turn my situation over to Him because it had become a hindrance.

When we go through difficult or challenging situations, it takes humility to be honest about our faults, weaknesses and shortcomings. I had to ask the Lord what He wanted me to learn from the identity theft. It was an enlightening experience for me and helped me to do some soul searching and get rid of the things that hindered my walk with God.

> "Ye did run well; who did hinder you that ye should not obey the truth?"
> *Galatians 5:7*

We may have been on the right track, but it's so easy to allow people or things to become hindrances to us. What or who is currently hindering you? What are you going to do about it? You can get so caught up with the things of this world and lose sight of your spiritual identity. You can place other things and people before your relationship with God. It's much harder to lose sight of what you can see (your material possessions and loved ones), but easy to lose sight of what you can't see (your spiritual identity).

Finally, you must turn your burdens over to the Lord rather than trying to deal with them on your own. The Word tells you to lay aside all the things that weigh you down spiritually.

> "Wherefore seeing we also are compassed about with so great a cloud of witnesses, let us lay aside every weight, and the sin which doth so easily beset us, and let us run with patience the race that is set before us,"
>
> *Hebrews 12:1*

You picked up the "weights," so it's up to you to lay them down. The weights are not sin, but the things that hold you down until the sin catches up to you. The Lord wants you to give all of those weights to Him to handle, so you can run your race with patience. You can't fix your situation anyway, so why do you carry those heavy burdens around? God already knows exactly what you're going through. He sees your failures, your disappointments, your hurts, your pain, your temptations and your frustrations. You need to give all of these things to the Lord and take on His yoke.

> "Take my yoke upon you, and learn of me; for I am meek and lowly in heart: and ye shall find rest unto your souls. For my yoke is easy, and my burden is light."
>
> *Matthew 11:29-30*

When you take on His yoke, you have to choose to exchange your heavy burdens for His light burden. Once you start walking on the lighter side of life, you will finally find rest for your soul. As you get closer to God, the better you will understand your spiritual identity and be able to embrace it. After your search for who you are, you need to be clear on why you are here on this earth.

Chapter 6

In Pursuit of Your Purpose

Once you've done an initial search of your spiritual identity, you need to understand how what you found relates to your purpose and destiny. A major part of this journey is the pursuit of your purpose, which may cause you to wonder why you are here and lead you on the path to finding out. When your spiritual identity is stolen, you may end up on a road where you are constantly searching for meaning and seeking approval from others. If you desire to know who you were created to be, it's essential that you understand your purpose. You have to be able to answer the question, "Why are you here?" If you're shaky about who you are, you won't be able to correctly answer that question. Until you can, you will never fully comprehend why you even exist or the reason you get up in the morning. You may even wonder why you were put on this earth. In turn, you won't be able to fully walk in your true purpose.

Why Are You Here?

As you continue to search your spiritual identity, this is the perfect opportunity to get clarity on your God-given purpose. If you are serious about finding out who you really are, you will find yourself in the middle of God's waiting process. You didn't lose your identity overnight, and you won't recover it overnight. It's a process that you must go through at some point in your life. You can't go around it or under it, but have to go *through* it.

Part II of my book, *Willing to Wait*, emphasizes the importance of preparation during your "season of waiting." While you are waiting to find yourself, a key part of the process involves dealing with your individual "issues." Those issues are the things that hinder you from reaching your full potential, such as self-doubt, fear, insecurity, self-righteousness, pride or low self-esteem. Chapter 5 of *Willing to Wait* discusses the importance of embracing your process and understanding your purpose while dealing with your issues. Finding your unique life purpose can be a very insightful journey of self-discovery. I want to be clear that your purpose doesn't mean your job. However, you may believe it is when your identity is tied to what you do, but it does not define your purpose. Although your circumstances may change throughout your life, your purpose should remain constant.

If you are going through a spiritual identity crisis, it can hold you back from fulfilling your purpose. The term "purpose" means the reason that something exists. You must understand your purpose because it affects the intended direction of your life. If you don't know who you are, how can you know why you are here? You are not here by accident, so you have to allow God to reveal the reason for your existence. Anything that is outside of your purpose will eventually become a distraction and take you off of your pre-ordained course. Only when you are connected to your spiritual identity can you live a "purpose-driven" life.

Dr. Myles Monroe is one of my favorite authors on the topic of purpose. In his book, *The Pursuit of Purpose*, he stated that the key to personal fulfillment is "purpose," which helps us to become who we were born to be. This is so true and is the reason why we can't give up on getting our stolen identity back. I love the simple yet powerful statement that Dr. Monroe made, "If you don't know the purpose of a thing, you will abuse it." The term, "abuse," simply means abnormal use. If you don't know the purpose of your spiritual identity, you will abuse it. In other words, you won't use it for its intended use. If you don't know your purpose in life, you will also abuse it. You will end up stuck in your identity crisis and trying to find your way out.

To help in your search for purpose, you must know that God made you exactly who you are and had a plan for your life from the beginning. You didn't decide when you would be born or who your parents would be. God made those decisions before you were even born because He actually knows why you are here. We've already talked about Joseph's story in the Bible. Once God revealed to him in a dream why he was there, he was able to discover his spiritual identity and fulfill his divine purpose.

In contrast, a good biblical example of someone who was searching for her identity and purpose is the

Samaritan woman. She is known as the "woman at the well," in the book of *John 4*.

> "The woman saith unto him, I know that Messias cometh, which is called Christ: when he is come, he will tell us all things. Jesus saith unto her, I that speak unto thee am he...The woman then left her waterpot, and went her way into the city, and saith to the men, Come, see a man, which told me all things that ever I did: is not this the Christ?"
> *John 4:25-26, 28-29*

This is a powerful story of personal transformation. The woman didn't know who she was because she identified with her problem, rather than who she was created to be. We don't know her name and are not given a lot of information about her. However, we do know that she was married five times and was currently shacking up with a man, so she probably had a reputation as being a "loose" woman in her city. She appeared at the well each day at 12 noon, which was the hottest time of day, when no one was there. She was clearly thirsty for more than water and was apparently in search of her identity and purpose.

Jesus pursued this woman with a past, though she didn't do anything to earn His attention. She was performing her daily task of getting water from the well. She was a mess of a woman meeting a Messiah of a Man, like many of us were before we were saved. While drawing her water she was presented with an opportunity to receive the "living water" offered by Jesus (*John 4:10*). She came to the well to do one job, but she was given another one after encountering Jesus. She was carrying her last hope for change in the waterpot. She had no time to prepare, no letter of invitation, no prior telephone call and no fax. She was alone at the well with Jesus. She had the chance to take the next step toward finding her spiritual identity, which began with the revelation of who God is and later who she is.

The woman couldn't receive salvation until she faced her sin and admitted the truth about her life. She also couldn't be saved until she knew the Savior because she didn't even know who she was worshipping. She initially saw Jesus only as a Jew and a prophet, but not the Messiah. She had to accept the truth about Jesus' life first.

This was a defining moment in her life when she decided to face herself and Jesus. At that point, she realized that she was a woman of worth and her past would not be held against her. She now had something important to share with the people in the city. She left her waterpot, which represented the things in her life that used to satisfy her. Then, she went into the city, which was the start of the journey toward her purpose. She immediately ran back to convince the people to return with her to the well to meet Jesus. They saw the change in her life, and it got their attention. She was no longer hiding at the well, but she was hurrying to it. Although her situation had not changed, she changed. We don't know the end of her story. Did she change her living arrangements? Settle down? Have kids? However, she made a decision to live a life of purpose. Once she discovered who she was in Christ, she began to immediately walk in her purpose. In order to do so, she had to go in a new direction.

Likewise, God knows the reason that you are here, and He wants you to also know. Once you know, then you can fulfill your ordained purpose. Understanding your purpose is critical to getting through your waiting process while you search to find yourself. If you don't know your purpose, you will never know who you are, why you are here or how you fit into God's plan. It's time for you to start walking in your God-given purpose, so you will be clear on the direction you're going in your life.

Where Are You Going?

When your spiritual identity has been compromised, not only will you not fully understand why you are here, but you will also be confused about where you're going. It doesn't matter where you've been, but rather where you're going. The direction of your life is guided by your "destiny," which is a predetermined course of events. Your destiny simply means your ultimate destination, which is the place that all of us should be striving to get to. Your destiny goes hand in hand with your purpose. While your purpose explains why you're here, your destiny tells you where you're going. God has a divine purpose and destiny for your life. He knows the plans that He has in store for your life (*Jeremiah 29:11*).

I had a dream about losing my car that gave me a whole new perspective on my destiny. I was sitting in my car, but I got out of it to look for something. When I tried to return to my car, I couldn't find it. It had disappeared into thin air. I was distressed and began to frantically look for my car, but I never could find it. Without my car, I was left stranded and had no way to get to my destination. I later realized that the car in the dream was symbolic of my destiny. The car represented the means for me to get to "my destination." In order for me to reach my destiny, I had to find my car. The Lord revealed to me that I had lost sight of my true destiny and was on a course to find it, and this is the case for many of us. However, the key question is how to figure out the way that we're supposed to be going.

When I recently took my car in for service, I received some additional insight on my destiny. When I dropped off my car, my service advisor provided me a loaner car. Once I got to work, I realized that I had left my laptop at home. When I was headed back home to get it, I couldn't find my house keys. I figured that I had left the keys in my car, but I couldn't find them when I went back to the dealership. I was wondering how I was going to get into my house without my keys. Since my garage remote is programmed into my car, I can't open my garage when I'm not in my car. After a thorough search of my car, I was happy to find my extra garage remote. Then, I was finally on my way home on the Sam Houston Toll Road. However, after I went through the EZ Tag lane, I realized that my EZ Tag was in my car. I immediately went to the EZ Tag store to pay for the violation and added the loaner car to my account. At this point, I was totally disoriented and frustrated. I didn't think about all the things that were in my car that I needed. It dawned on me that I needed my own car to get to my "appointed" destination. Like me, many of us are in "temporary" cars in our lives and are wondering why we are having so many road blocks to reaching our destination. Moreover, we may know where we should be at this point in our lives, but don't know how or have the means to get there.

Even when we get to our destination, there are things in our cars that give us access to the things that belong to us. As a result, we need to return the "loaner" cars in our lives because they can only take us where we need to go on a short-term basis. In order to reach our pre-determined destination, we must get back into the "car" that God has reserved for each of us. When we're in our own car, not only can we reach our destination, but we will also have the "keys" to access the treasures that He has in store for us. What a deep revelation! I could not wait to get back into my car, so that I would be back on the road to my destiny.

Sometimes many of us know exactly where we are supposed to be going, but we choose not to go that way. For example, God gave Jonah clear instructions on where he was supposed to go, but he decided to go in another direction. However, God has a way of reminding us of where we're supposed to be going. Jonah had to be thrown overboard and laid in the belly of the whale for three days before he decided to obey God. The whale spit him out at the place where he had originally started. God was telling him to return to the starting line and to go where He told him to go. When he told Jonah to go to Nineveh, he did not have an option. He told Jonah to go northeast to Nineveh by land, and he went west by sea on the way to Tarshish.

When we seek to run away from the presence and call of God, we have usually lost sight of our destiny. We can't try to get to our destiny by taking a different route from God. The Lord will tell us to do something, and we decide not to obey for some reason. We try to figure out the "why, when and how" of what God is doing instead of trusting that He knows what's best for us. Remember that obedience is better than sacrifice (*1 Samuel 15:22*). Don't try to do anything extra or what you think is best, but what God told you to do. The anointing is on the instructions, so it's critical that we follow them. When the Lord has a call or purpose for your life, you can run, but you can't hide. David said it best, if he ascended up to heaven or made his bed in hell, God would also be there (*Psalm 139:8*). As you know, God is omnipresent, so your attempted escape from Him is futile. You can't play hide and seek with the Lord because He will always find you.

Some of us are just like Jonah, and we know exactly where God has told us to go. Once we have clear directions from God, we are held accountable. When we don't follow them, we are in outright disobedience. I have a friend whom the Lord had to take through a "Jonah experience" to get him to make a move. However, he eventually did move, but he went to the wrong place. My friend had been stuck in the past, and the Lord was trying to expand his territory. Sadly, he knew that it was not where he was supposed to be, but he kept trying to convince himself otherwise. The Lord has allowed his "brook" to dry up, but he is still being disobedient. I told him not to be surprised if he opens his door and a big whale is sitting out there. Regardless of all the things that he's done to prolong the inevitable, he can rest assured that he will eventually have to go to "his" Nineveh. Many of us are just like my friend, but we can take comfort in the fact that our steps have already been ordered by the Lord (*Psalm 37:23*). We will get to our place of destiny, but we can be the one to hold up what God has for us. All we have to do is to get to the place called "there," which is where our provision is already waiting on us. Like God did with Elijah, He is telling some of you that your brook has dried up (*1 Kings 17:7*), and it's time to move to your place called "there." If you stay "here," you will never be able to get "there."

On the other extreme, many people are totally clueless about where they are going. They don't know where they are now, so they definitely have no idea where they are supposed to be going. They couldn't find their destiny if it was staring them in the face. In fact, they are sure to take the wrong turn at some point in their lives. These wandering souls may have a life map, but it's taking them to the wrong destination. They may know the right destination, but they have the wrong map -- one that they drew up. If you are on the way to

New York, would you follow a map to California? If you haven't figured it out, you will never reach your destination with that approach. When I was going in the wrong direction years ago, the Lord had to get my attention and remind me of where I was supposed to be going. It wasn't that I was doing bad things, but I was not doing what the Lord told me to do. I was doing some "good" things supposedly in the name of God, but they were not what He told me to do. Because of my identity crisis, I was too busy trying to please people rather than God. Sometimes, our own choices will cause us to go into a different direction than we should. Moreover, oftentimes other people will tap into our lives and cause us to go in the wrong direction. However, regardless of how we started down the wrong path, it's never too late to turn around.

When I was a girl scout, we used a compass to determine if we were going in the right direction. However, now, most people depend on a more high tech version - a navigation system or GPS - to help them get from point A to point B. They don't even bother writing down directions or printing them out from MapQuest anymore. They just punch in the address on the navigation system or GPS and trust the device to do the rest. However, the directions are only as good as the maps in the system. I recently met a friend for lunch who had used her GPS to meet me. She said that it had stopped about 200 feet before reaching the restaurant. I asked her, "How do you get to your destination if the system doesn't work and you don't have the directions?" She said that she was close enough to find the place, so she just drove around in circles until she found it. That's why I don't rely on my navigation system, but I prefer to print out a hard copy of the directions before I go anywhere that I have never been before. If we have clear directions, we can get to our destination much quicker and with fewer stops.

Do you honestly know where you are going in your life? Do you have clear directions from God on how to reach your destination? Or are you relying on your own or someone else's roadmap? As you know, you can never trust that your natural compasses will work for you all the time. You may think you're going north, when in fact you are going south. However, when it comes to your spiritual compass, the Bible, you can't go wrong if you follow the directions.

> "Thy word is a lamp unto my feet, and a light unto my path."
>
> *Psalm 119:105*

The Word will not only give you the directions for your life, but it will also light up the right path for you. All you have to do is walk out the path that the Lord has already paved for you.

Even when we finally figure out where we're going, we can be so focused on reaching our destination that we don't enjoy the journey. The fun part is the individual journey that God has ordained for each of our lives. My journey will be different from your journey, and yours will be different from anyone else's. Since our lives can easily become routine, we can lose focus on the direction of our lives. Some people are always living for the mountaintop, but sometimes we have to come down to the valley. They work so hard to get a promotion, but then they don't have time to spend with their family. For example, a person may work two jobs to take care of their kids, but they don't even have time to see them. We should enjoy the journey rather than focus on getting to the destination. If you're on the right road, you will eventually make it to your destination. So, you might as well take the scenic route toward finding your spiritual identity.

When Satan steals your spiritual identity, his goal is to make you doubt not only who you are, but to question where you are going. You can't reach your full potential if you lack your spiritual identity because you will be confused or doubtful about where you're supposed to go. Since your destiny is predetermined, all you need to do is to walk it out according to God's will. You can rest assured that the Lord has ordered your steps and your stops. It's essential that you know where you are now, where you need to be and how to get there. Don't let the enemy detour you and keep you from getting to your ordained destination any longer. Now that you've done your identity search, you need to take a closer look at what you've found.

STEP 2
Review Questions

1) Do you think your spiritual identity needs protecting from the enemy? Are you taking any steps to protect it? If not, what steps do you need to take now?

2) Have you done a search of your spiritual identity? Are you happy about where you are at this point in your life? Do you feel as if you should be further along? If so, what's holding you back (e.g., job, relationships, fear, friends, etc.)? Why?

3) Do you know who God created you to be? Compare it to who you think you are now. What are the differences? What areas do you feel need to change? Or stay the same?

4) Have you done a spiritual inventory of your life? Where are you most vulnerable to the enemy's attacks? What areas do you need to work on? When are you going to start?

5) Have you willingly or unknowingly given your spiritual identity away? Can you recall specific incidents in your life where pieces of your identity were taken from you (be specific)? Are you taking action to recover any losses you experienced?

6) Have you discovered God's purpose for your life? Do you believe that you are here for a reason? If so, are you walking in your purpose? How is your purpose connected to your spiritual identity?

STEP 3

INSPECT
All The Findings

"He that findeth his life shall lose it: and he that loseth his life for my sake shall **find** it."
Matthew 10:39

POETIC EXHORTATION
All The Findings

You have to inspect all of your findings,

And look closer when your life's unwinding,

You need to check out all of your sources,

And recognize the invisible stealing forces,

All of your pockets need to be checked,

If you haven't found all that's missing yet.

STEP 3
Overview

The third step in the process of recovering your stolen identity is to <u>inspect</u> the findings from your initial inventory. To "inspect" means to examine carefully and critically, especially for flaws. In this step, you are in phase two of your inventory process, where you need to do a thorough inspection of what you've found out during your preliminary search. Your spiritual identity search should have turned up general information about what has been stolen from you, so you need to examine it closely to confirm what's really missing in your life. It's necessary for you to take a closer look at your findings to get more specific details about your identity theft. The deeper you dig, the more you will learn about your actual loss and what you'll need to get back.

Similarly, when you get ready to buy a house, it's critical that you do a thorough inspection. The purpose of the inspection is to uncover visible and hidden defects in the house, which may be a sign of a bigger problem. From the outside, the house may look great. However, until you fully inspect the inside of the house, you don't have enough facts to make an informed decision about whether to buy it or not. During your inspection, you have to take a closer look at every room in the house to find things like cracks in the sheetrock or broken tiles. Some problems may be less obvious than others, so the burden is on you to examine the house very carefully. Otherwise, you could miss some major problems. It's a good idea to also have a professional inspection done if needed. Before I bought my house, I remember the tedious inspection process, where I went room by room pointing out any issues before the closing. Similarly, when you are inspecting the findings related to your stolen identity, you need to look very closely so you don't overlook any missing pieces.

REFLECTIONS ON
Identity Theft

"When someone hijacks a consumer's identity, it can be a nightmare."

Jodie Bernstein
Director of the FTC's Bureau of Consumer Protection

"The victims can even be infants. If you have a social security number, you can be a victim of identity theft."

Melodi Gates

Chapter 7

Check Out Your Sources

After you've completed the search for yourself, you must then determine the sources that your spiritual identity is connected to. Whether the spiritual identity thief can get access to your identity depends on its source. A "source" is the point of origin. Your identity can originate from a natural or a spiritual source (see Table 2). If your identity is tied to your job, credit or finances, it has a natural source. Since that source is only temporary, we know that our natural identity is at risk of being stolen. On the contrary, if our identity is connected to Christ, it has a spiritual source that is eternal. In this case, our identity is still at risk, but it can only be taken if we forfeit it or let go of it. That's why it's essential that you check out your "sources."

When our spiritual identities are I-jacked by the enemy, we become diminished versions of who God created us to be. As you know, spiritual identity theft occurs when we draw our identity from a source other than who we are in Christ. When we assume the identity of what we do, either at work, home or church, our well being is held captive to how well we perform. If our identity is based on what we have, we are also held hostage by how much we have or don't have. However, when our identity is secure in Christ, we have a reliable and unchanging source of meaning. When we attach our identity to His unchanging nature, our "real identity" can never be taken from us and is not dependent on other people or our circumstances. We would have to give it up to the enemy, whether it's voluntarily or not. Therefore, we must refuse to let go of our spiritual identities by disconnecting them from our true Source and connecting them to a source that we can't rely on.

Unreliable Sources

During the inventory of our lives, we must confirm if our identity is tied to an "unreliable source." In other words, we can't put our trust in this type of source. However, our identities long to connect to a secondary source until we find our primary source, Jesus Christ. If we allow our identities to be tied to the "world" (an unreliable source), we will never fully know who we are. The word, "world," is derived from the Greek word, "kosmos," which means an orderly system. When we look at the world today, it looks anything but orderly. On the contrary, it looks very chaotic and confusing from where I'm standing. The "world" is intended to generally refer to this world's system that's under the influence of the "prince of the power of the air" (*Ephesians 2:2*). As we can see, Satan is running the world's show and that's why the world is against the ways of God and His people. This is the main reason that the world is not a reliable source.

Jesus didn't get His identity from the world, and neither can we. When He was here in the flesh, the world didn't even know who He was. In fact, His very own received Him not.

> "He was in the world, and the world was made by him, and the world knew him not. He came unto his own, and his own received him not."
> *John 1:10-11*

If the world couldn't figure out who Jesus is, why should we be concerned about whether or not they know who we are? If you are expecting the world to know who you are in Christ, you are wasting your time. What you can expect from the world is rejection, hatred and jealousy. The world tries to make you believe that you are not worthy unless you live by its standards. That's why you can't try to get your identity from the world. The world looks at us as peculiar people, which is what we are. In turn, the world will never understand who we really are or why we don't fit into its system.

Another problem occurs when we start believing what the world thinks about us, rather than who God has already said we are. We often want to be accepted and valued by the world, so we buy into its beliefs without regard to God's will for our lives. When we look to the world to recognize who we are and give us a pat on the back, it will lead us into worldly thinking. Then, we'll find ourselves in a state of spiritual amnesia because we lose track of who we are supposed to be. However, we must avoid the temptation to conform to the world's way of thinking.

> "And be not conformed to this world: but be ye transformed by the renewing of your mind, that ye may prove what is that good, and acceptable, and perfect, will of God."
>
> *Romans 12:2*

In this scripture, Paul warns us to be transformed (changed) by renewing our minds. It implies that we have to take action to "renew," which means to make our minds new. The more we study and meditate on the Word and learn God's way of thinking, the less conformed we will be to this world. We can't allow the world to try to squeeze us into its mold because it wants to shape what we think of ourselves. We must understand that it's a "mind" thing. Until you change your thinking to God's way of thinking, you will not be empowered to do the perfect will of God. If you don't dismiss the world's beliefs about you, then you will be stuck in a revolving spiritual identity crisis. If you want to overcome such crisis, you can't worry about who the world thinks you are. Instead, stand on the Word and rest in who Christ says you are. Otherwise, you will end up looking to the wrong source for your identity.

Despite being tempted several times by Satan in the wilderness, Jesus remained confident that God was His sole source. When Jesus was baptized, God declared, "This is my beloved Son in whom I am well pleased" (*Matthew 3:17*). Not only did Jesus say who He was, God also said who He was. Following the baptism, the Holy Spirit led Jesus into the wilderness to be tempted.

> "And when he had fasted forty days and forty nights, he was afterward an hungered. And when the tempter came to him, he said, If thou be the Son of God, command that these stones be made bread. But he answereth and said, It is written, Man shall not

live by bread alone, but by every word that proceedeth out of the mouth of God."

Matthew 4:2-4

After Jesus had fasted for 40 days and nights, He was naturally hungry. However, He knew exactly who He was and whose He was, the Son of God. He also knew why he was there (His purpose) and where He was going (His destiny). Satan questioned Jesus' identity by asking, "If thou be the Son of God..." He wanted Jesus to doubt who He is, to discard His identity (based on God's truth) and to establish His own identity (based on His abilities). Satan thought he could tempt Jesus to forget who He was by offering Him something that He already had – power. Satan is apparently a little slow since he tried to offer "some power" to the One who has "all power." Even though Jesus had the power to turn the stones to bread, He chose instead to rely on His ultimate Source, God. If the enemy attacked Jesus' identity, you know he is going after yours as a follower of Him. No matter what temptation comes your way, your Source is available to sustain you. When Satan tries to bring doubt, fear, unbelief or self-pity your way, you have to stay connected to God, the true Source of your identity.

You should have a new revelation of who you are now and who you're supposed to be. If you are not sure where you need to be, you should examine the source of your identity. If you don't know *who* you are, you won't understand *whose* you are. If God is your source, that's where you will look for direction in your life. If your identity is tied to Christ, you have a reliable source that will not move on you. However, if your source is the world, that's where your identity will be connected. As you know, it's an unreliable source. That's why one day you're up and the next day you're down. To counter this problem, you need to continue to check to make sure your identity is connected to the right Source.

It's All "In Christ"

We all know what represents our natural identity, like our name, address and social security number, but do we know the extent of our spiritual identity in Christ? What if you applied for a credit card or mortgage loan, but were denied for some unknown reason? Although you have excellent credit and pay all your bills on time, it doesn't matter if a con artist steals your identity and runs up debts that you don't know about. That's the reality of the world that we live in now. Moreover, it is also a part of our spiritual world, which is why it's so important that we know in whom or what our identity is anchored at all times. There are many different sources that our identities will try to connect to until we find Christ. Even when we find Him, we still have to keep checking to make sure our identities stays connected to Him. Once who we are is settled, we can find our true purpose and fulfill our destiny. We no longer have to maintain a "stolen" identity because we have the "real" one.

Do you know your spiritual PIN? Not for use with your debit or ATM card, but as a follower of Christ. This is what grants you access to who you are in Christ. We need to verify our identities and be sure that we know who we are and what belongs to us. Are you ready to enter your PIN into your spiritual ATM while the enemy is carefully looking over your shoulder to steal your spiritual identity? Your relationship with Christ identifies you with Him, and nothing else matters. Your true identity is not based on your feelings, how much you know, what you do or what others say about you. Don't allow the enemy to rob you of your God-given identity another day.

If you did the search for your identity in Chapter 4, you should have a good idea of what it is or is not connected to. Your identity will ultimately be tied to something or someone, which can change over time. At one point, your identity could be tied to your job, but years later it may be tied to your spouse. How you choose to define yourself will be dependent on what your identity is actually tied to at any given time. If the source of your identity is unstable, your identity will also be unstable. If the source of your identity is constantly fluctuating, you are bound to have an identity that is also constantly changing. However, if your identity is connected to a source that is secure and stable, you will find that your identity is also secure and stable.

The only truly unshakable foundation for your identity is Jesus Christ, and that's why your "real" identity is in Him. Only by fully identifying with Him will you be able to live the abundant life that He has already provided for you. In *Matthew 7*, Jesus tells the parable of the wise and foolish builders to illustrate the importance of your spiritual foundation.

> "Therefore whosoever heareth these sayings of mine, and doeth them, I will liken him unto a wise man, which built his house upon a rock: And the rain descended, and the floods came, and the winds blew, and beat upon that house; and it fell not: for it was founded upon a rock. And every one that heareth these sayings of mine, and doeth them not, shall be likened unto a foolish man, which built his house upon the sand: And the rain descended, and the floods came, and the winds blew, and beat upon that house; and it fell: and great was the fall of it."
>
> *Matthew 7:24-27*

In this scripture, Jesus warns us that it's not enough to just hear His Word, but we must also obey it. He compares a man who hears and obeys Him to a wise man who builds his house on a rock. When the floods and winds threatened the house, it remained intact because it was built on a secure base. Likewise, the only solid Rock on which we can build our spiritual house is Christ Himself. When we build our lives on the Rock, it is set on a solid, unshakeable foundation.

On the other hand, Jesus likens a man who hears but doesn't obey Him to a foolish man who built his house on sand. Of course, the house built on a movable surface, like sand, will fall when the storms come because it has an unstable foundation. In this parable, the houses represent our lives, and what we build them on is critical. Although both houses appear to look the same on the outside, their comparative stability differed greatly. It can be disastrous when the storms come if our lives are not built on a Rock foundation. We must build our houses differently, by hearing and doing God's Word. Otherwise, our lives will be at risk of being swept away. Is your spiritual house built on a solid foundation? If not, it's time for you to move unless you have a good flood insurance policy. It's a necessity that your "primary" identity is tied solely to God at all times.

I had a very profound dream, which gave me new insight on what it means to have my identity "in Christ." In the dream, I walked into a big room that looked like a jail with several cells in the back. When I looked up, I saw my books sitting on a shelf along with other things related to my life. While I was talking to someone in one of the jail cells, I was suddenly behind the bars myself. Anxiously thinking about how to get out, I pushed the bars and discovered that the door had been open the whole time. I was still afraid for some reason, and then a police officer came into the room. When I woke up, I was not sure what the dream meant. However, I later realized that it was related to my fear of losing my "identity" after my natural identity had been stolen.

When my identity was dependent on the things I did, such as being an author or attorney, I found myself in bondage (behind bars). However, when I discovered who I really am, the doors were unlocked and I was free to walk out. The puzzling part was that I still could not find my identity. After meditating on the dream, I received a powerful revelation. The reason that I could not find my identity was because someone had it – not the identity thief...but the Identity Giver (Christ). The Lord was letting me know that He had my identity now, so I no longer had to worry about it because He was holding it for safekeeping.

My spiritual identity as well as yours is hidden in Christ. When your identity is "in Christ," you can be assured that you will be exactly who you were created to be. No one can steal your identity when it's "totally" in Christ, not in the world. The enemy can't touch it unless you give the predator access to it.

However, many of us have already given Satan access to our identities because we don't fully know what it means to be "in Christ." To be "in Christ," we must first know who Christ is. If we don't know Him, we will never know who we are in Him. Once we know who we are "in Christ," we can truly discover who we really are and find meaning in something greater than ourselves. Unlike the world's view, your spiritual identity is not something that needs to be created or developed by you or anyone else. It's not contingent upon your relationships, possessions, successes, failures, etc. Your identity is totally linked to Christ and is ready to be claimed when you receive the salvation that He freely gives us. When you accept Him as your Lord and Savior, the Bible says that you are now "in Christ."

On the contrary, some people still think that they have to "work" to establish their relationship with Christ. The truth is that we are saved by grace through faith, not by our works.

> "For by grace are ye saved through faith; and that not of yourselves: it is the gift of God: Not of works, lest any man should boast."
>
> *Ephesians 2:8-9*

Our salvation is a gift from God and is not based on anything we have or have not done. Since it's not based on our "works," we can't boast or take any credit for it. Our relationship with God is simply because of what Christ did for us...period. Jesus gave His life for us and paid the price for our sins. In turn, we are able to experience this "new" nature because of what He did on the cross for us.

All we have to do is receive His gift of eternal life to be "in Christ." Moreover, we never have to worry about our spiritual identities again or having them stolen by Satan because they are secure in Him. However, that's the reason that Satan is constantly trying to attack our identities because he knows that they are off limits. He desires to make us doubt our spiritual identity and whether who we are in Christ is in fact "new." His attack on Adam and Eve focused specifically on their relationship with God (*Genesis 3:1-5*). As a result, he is hoping that we forfeit our spiritual identity and voluntarily hand it over without a fight like they did.

In order for us to fully walk in this new life, we need to explore what "in Christ" means and how it applies to our lives today. In scripture, the apostle Paul reminded us of our "new identity" in Christ.

> "Therefore if any man be in Christ, he is a new creature: old things are passed away; behold, all things are become new."
>
> 2 Corinthians 5:17

This scripture reaffirms that if we're "in Christ," we are "new" creatures and who we used to be no longer matters. Paul was the right person to talk about this transformation since he had switched from being a "persecutor of Christ" to being "in Christ." The phrase, "in Christ," was often used in his epistles to refer to a believer's spiritual relationship to Christ. To be in Christ is to be a "new creature," which is brought about by the indwelling of the Holy Spirit in those who believe in Christ. Not only do we have a new name, but we have a new spiritual nature. This change is so great that "old things are passed away," which includes our old thoughts, old beliefs, old attitudes and old actions. Whatever you did as an "old creature" (the things that you may still feel guilty about, can't forgive yourself for, or never want anyone to know about), the good news is that it's all in your past. So, leave it back where it belongs because you are a new creature. When you connect with Christ, those things in your past are gone and "all things are become new" in your life. Not just some things, but ALL things. Everything about you should become new. You have a new talk and a new walk that reflects your new relationship with Christ.

There are several biblical examples of people who found a "new" relationship in Christ that changed their sense of identity and the direction of their lives. For example, Matthew, a tax collector, had a life driven by greed until he was invited to follow Jesus (Matthew 9:9). Suddenly, he had a "new" identity when he chose to follow Him and became one of His disciples. There were also four fishermen, Peter, Andrew, James and John, who also changed when they left their fishing nets to follow Him and become fishers of men (Matthew 4:18-25). Things begin to change for the better when people hook up with Christ. Your life will also change when you embrace your new identity in Christ.

However, one way that Satan tries to steal your identity is by reminding you of your past. When you came to Jesus and invited Him into your life, you became a new creation. The person you used to be is gone. You may be in the same body, but you are brand new. So the next time Satan tries to remind you of your past, just remind him of your future and his.

As you embrace who you are in Christ, you need to understand the role that He plays in your life. You will discover that your thinking, your feelings and your behavior will change as you seek to exemplify what it means to be in Christ. Once we become identified with Christ, we are also crucified with Him.

> "I am crucified with Christ: nevertheless I live; yet not I, but Christ liveth in me: and the life which I now live in the flesh I live by the faith of the Son of God, who loved me, and gave himself for me."
> *Galatians 2:20*

This scripture describes the spiritual life of believers when we are in Christ. The "old" man was crucified along with Christ, but the "new" man lives because of our new identity in Christ. When we say we believe that Christ was crucified for us, we are also saying that we believe we were crucified with Him. As Christians, we should live in a state of dependence on Christ. Even though we live *in* the flesh, we don't live *after* the flesh. Those who have true faith will live according to that faith, which is based on Christ giving Himself for us. This is how we know Christ crucified. When we unite with Christ, we share in His death, burial and resurrection.

Many people believe that once they're saved, that everything in their lives will be smooth sailing. Once they accept Jesus Christ as their personal Savior, they think there's nothing left to do but sit back and wait for His return. Those folks think they don't have to worry about trials and tribulations, but that's the furthest thing from the truth. Just because we're saved doesn't mean that we won't go through tough times. When it comes to what we believe about ourselves, we may base it on our own abilities, who our parents are, our education or our position in the community – rather than Christ. Before you even had sense to know who you were or what you wanted to be, God had already predestined your life. God knew you before you knew you. He has already confirmed and secured your spiritual identity.

Now that you know the true Source of your identity, you can reclaim who you are in Christ. Once your identity is tied to Him, everything you need to live the abundant life is in and through Christ. When you're in Him, you have answers to your problems. By having access to Jesus' name, your spiritual obligations and debts have been paid in full. Whatever you go through, such as fear of rejection, failure or loneliness, is resolved when God sees you in Christ. Your struggle for meaning and value are no longer burdened by your own flawed efforts. In God's eyes, no one is more important or secure than you after you entrust your life to His Son.

Now that you know what it means to be in Christ, do you think you are an old, dying creature or a new, living creature in Him? You're not trying to shake off your "old" life because that has already passed away. You have a completely "new" life. All things are new when you are in Christ. That's who you really are, and you need to believe it and make it real in your life.

Get A Life!

When we talk about the meaning of "life," most of us probably think about material things and people who are tied to our "natural" life. When I was in law school, my whole life was consumed with reading cases and studying for exams. I lived at the University of Houston Law Center and only went home to sleep for a few hours each night. This was a repetitive cycle for me. My family and friends couldn't understand that I didn't have time to talk on the phone, go to dinner or hang out at the mall. However, after I finished law school and passed the bar exam, I didn't know what to do with my life. I suddenly had all of this extra time on my hands, but I just continued to go to work and back home. I remember a friend of mine telling me to "Get a life!" I agreed that it was time for me to start enjoying my life, so I began a search for fun activities that would make my life more fulfilling. However, it dawned on me that I already had a life...an "abundant life" promised by Jesus Christ, but I just needed to tap into it.

If we want to understand the true meaning of life, we must have a clear understanding of *John 10:10*. This is the key scripture that the Lord gave me when I first began studying the concept of spiritual identity theft. Let's take a closer look at what this scripture states:

> "The thief cometh not, but for to **steal**, and to kill, and to destroy: I am come that they might have life, and that they might have it more abundantly."
>
> *John 10:10*

Before we can grasp its full meaning, we need to look at the context of chapter 10 of the book of John. In prior verses, Jesus told the parable of the shepherd and the sheep and revealed Himself as the Good Shepherd over His sheep.

> "Then said Jesus unto them again, Verily, verily, I say unto you, I am the door of the sheep. All that ever came before me are thieves and robbers: but the sheep did not hear them."
>
> *John 10:7-8*

Jesus spoke of himself as the "gate" of the sheep. During biblical times, a shepherd kept his sheep in a fenced area at night to protect them from wild animals. Once all the sheep were safely inside, the shepherd would sit down in the open gate. A thief would not try to enter in through the gate, but would instead climb over the fence to try to "steal" a sheep. Jesus said that some of the religious leaders (the Pharisees) were like the thieves and robbers. They didn't really love the people, but only wanted to get what they could from them. This is the same tactic that Satan uses against believers today, and of course he uses the people closest to us, like our spouses, parents, children, friends, and even our enemies, to do his dirty work.

Now that we have a better idea of who the "thief" described in *John 10:10* is, we need to find out what he is really after in that scripture. The thief comes for no other reason "but for to steal, and to kill, and to destroy" the sheep. Although the thief's main goal was to steal the sheep, he was willing to also kill and destroy them if necessary, just like today's criminals. Even now, a thief's motive is always the same - to get something for nothing and to destroy anyone or anything that gets in his or her way. Likewise, Satan takes the same approach when he tries to steal our spiritual identities.

In sharp contrast, Jesus, as the Good Shepherd, didn't come to destroy the sheep like the thieves and robbers, but rather He said, "I am come that they might have life..." Since Jesus was very familiar with the thief and what he wanted, He came to do something to stop him. He made a very powerful statement about giving "life" in *John 10:10*, so we need to explore what kind of life He was talking about. There are additional scriptures where He clarifies the life He meant. Particularly, Jesus has said many times that He is the giver of life. He said in *John 11:25*, "I am the resurrection and the *life*." Later in *John 14:6*, He stated, "I am the way, the truth, and the *life*." I think the "I" in those verses is intended to be emphatic and means that life is found only in Him. To receive this kind of "eternal life" that comes from knowing Christ (*John 17:3*), we must understand the special relationship that exists between a shepherd and his sheep. He said that His sheep know His voice and will not follow a stranger.

Now that we know the kind of life Jesus came to give us, we need to examine what He meant by giving life "more abundantly." Before we begin to have visions about the material things, like the new houses and cars or the raise, we need to consider what this "abundant" life means. Jesus didn't just come to give life, but He goes on to quantify the kind of life. The question is whether the "abundantly" should be taken literally. What is considered "abundant" for one person may be inadequate for another person, so it would require a subjective interpretation. The Greek word for "abundant" is "perisson," which means "overflowing," "superabundant," or "over and above a certain quantity." In effect, Jesus promises us an abundant life, which is eternal and far better than we could ever envision.

If that's the case, why are we always trying to reduce life down to a size that we can measure? If we didn't have a reason to live, life would become a meaningless repetition of activities. When King Solomon looked at all of his material possessions, he said it best that "all is vanity" (*Ecclesiastes 1:2*). However, when we have a purpose to live, life takes on a new meaning and we have a reason to get up in the morning. So, it's natural for most people to seek to "get a life" if they don't have one. However, so often they search for meaning in their jobs, their families, their possessions, etc. While these are not bad places to seek "life," they are just not the best place to find the "abundant life" that Jesus offers. Only in Him will we find that kind of life, so all of us need to "get a life." Since Satan knows about this abundant life that we have in Christ, he wants to do everything he can to steal it from us and kill and destroy us spiritually in the process. However, with the knowledge of the life that we have been graciously given, we can stop the enemy from stealing our spiritual identities.

TABLE 2
The Key Sources of Your Identity

RELIABLE SOURCE
JESUS CHRIST **(Only Primary Source)** +spiritual source +based on your relationship to Christ +internally dependent +secure and unchanging

UNRELIABLE SOURCES
THE WORLD **(Secondary Sources)** -natural sources -based on your relationship with others -externally dependent -unstable and changing

Family Roles	Jobs	Relationships
Titles	Wealth	Possessions

Chapter 8

Check All Your Pockets

Now that you have done an assessment of the real source of your own identity, you need to do a thorough inventory of what's been stolen from you. In order to do so, you need to know if your identity is tied to anything other than Christ. When you look to these other sources, you are in effect allowing Satan to pick your pocket and steal your spiritual identity. To "pick somebody's pocket" means to steal from someone's pockets or bag without him or her noticing. For example, a thief in a crowded subway may pick your pocket and take your wallet without you knowing.

Sometimes the term, "check your pockets," is intended to mean that you need to look for something valuable that may be hidden there. For example, I recently saw a news article entitled, *Check Your Pockets for National Lottery Ticket*, which grabbed my attention. A U.K. National Lottery win of £2.5 million was still unclaimed and lottery officials were urging players to check their pockets for the winning ticket. The winner had not come forward to claim it. I don't play the lottery, but it's interesting that someone had won the jackpot and apparently didn't know it.

As believers, we have won a "spiritual jackpot," but some of us need to check our pockets to reaffirm the treasures that we have received as followers of Christ. I recall when I put on an old pair of jeans that I had not worn in a while and discovered that I had a $20 bill in my pocket, which was a pleasant surprise. The reality is that the money had been there the whole time, but I didn't discover it until I checked my pockets. Likewise, we all have valuable stuff in our "spiritual pockets" that still need to be discovered.

In the context of identity theft, the term "check your pockets" implies that a thief may have secretly stolen your "identity" out of your figurative pockets. There may have been items (e.g., money, credit, etc.) that you expected to be in your pockets, but you later found out they were missing. This is exactly what happens with our identities when they are seized by a pickpocket. We need to understand how the pickpocket operates to better grasp how easily he or she gets access to our stuff.

A few years ago, I was on vacation in Italy and knew the danger of pickpockets. As a result, I didn't carry a purse or wallet and hid my money in a hidden pouch that was not easily accessible. I figured if a thief could get to my pouch, he or she would have worked hard enough to earn it. The streets were very congested, so I instinctively checked my pockets every time someone bumped into me. While I was walking with a group of people, a woman right next to me had her wallet stolen from her bag by a pickpocket in a matter of seconds. She didn't even know that the thief had her wallet until it was too late. She was upset because no one told her what was happening. However, she was the only one who could check her pockets because she's the only one who knew what was in it.

Did you even realize that you had fallen prey to a pickpocket? Since Satan is a skilled pickpocket, most of us may not even know that our spiritual identities have been slipped out of our spiritual pockets. Have you checked your pockets lately? You may be surprised at what you find or don't find. Your proverbial "pockets" are symbolic of your spiritual identity. When you check your pockets, you are effectively doing an inventory of the missing pieces of the puzzle of your life, which we talked about earlier. You are looking to see what your identity is tied to, which is whatever you're tied to. If you're tied to Christ, you should have everything that you're entitled to in your pockets, but the pickpocket (Satan) may have secretly slipped some things out. If your identity is tied to the world, it's safe to say you may have more missing from your pockets than you ever realized.

Consequently, you must be prepared to do some soul searching to find out if your spiritual identity is in fact tied to sources other than Christ. You can so easily start basing your identity on what you do instead of who you are. A good way to tell what a person's identity is tied to is to observe what he or she is consumed with. What does he or she spend most of his or her time doing? What's their normal day based around? Is it God centered or world centered? You can try to fool yourself by making all kinds of excuses, but whatever consumes your life will eventually have a hold on your identity.

Do you know you can make "idols" out of worldly ambitions? An "idol" is anything that you put before God in your life. It's not just limited to material things, but it can also include people. Of course, you should love your family and enjoy what you do at work, but you need to have the right balance. If you did an inventory of your life right now, what would you find? What does most of your life revolve around? This is an important question that we all need to ask ourselves and be honest about the answer.

Satan's ultimate identity theft starts with the lie that your worth is determined by your performance and others' opinions about you. This results in the loss of your God-given identity, which bases your worth on God's truth about you. You have to know that God expressed your true worth by the value He placed upon you in creation and by the price Jesus paid for your redemption at the cross. As a result, Satan goes after your identity by focusing mainly on three areas of vulnerability: 1) people, 2) possessions and 3) positions (see Table 3). The truth is that real life is not found in what I call the "3 P's," but it's so easy for you to look to these sources to find your real identity. If you trust people, possessions or positions to do for you what only God can do, these things can become "idols" in your life. Furthermore, you will usually end up disappointed because even when you have them, you are still not satisfied or sure about who you are. The reason is because your "real" identity can only be found in Jesus Christ.

In order to find yourself, you have to confirm whether your identity (who you are) is tied to one or more of the

3 P's. We will address each category separately. However, all of them are inter-related and may have some overlap.

PEOPLE TIES

One of the key ways to have our spiritual identities stolen involve people (including ourselves), and this is a key area where we have allowed the enemy to steal from us. We tend to carry the burdens of people with whom we have relationships (e.g., parents, spouses, siblings, children, etc.). We have had to overcome many obstacles to get where we are in our lives, so we can't allow people to rob us of our God-given identities, especially when it comes to relationships and our appearance.

Robbed by Relationships

The enemy has been doing a good job of robbing us through our relationships. The type of relationship is not important, whether it's with your spouse or friend. Because we were created to be relational beings, this is an area where Satan works through people to cause us to lose our identities. This is an area where we are being robbed blind when we allow people to become our "source" rather than Jesus. We can't put our trust in man because he or she will let us down most of the time.

The reasons that we are duped by the enemy in the area of relationships can be narrowed down to the following three areas, which I call the "3 A's":

1) <u>Affection:</u> Whether you are single or married, you may be looking for someone to complete you or make you feel better about yourself. You just want

someone to love you for who you are and treat you like you think you deserve to be treated. You were made to desire love and companionship, so it's not a bad thing unless you allow your identity to be tied to a spouse, boyfriend, girlfriend, significant other or special person. This may be an unhealthy soul tie, which causes you to be unsure about who you are. If the person leaves you, then you start to question who you are. Anytime you have to toss your identity out to be involved with someone, whether it's a spouse, loved one or friend, there's a serious problem. Your identity is not based on your marital status, so it doesn't matter if you are single, married or divorced. If your identity is rightly connected to Christ, your identity should not change when people come in and out of your life. You may be hurt or disappointed by their actions, but you should be able to move on because you know who you are in Christ. We've all heard the old cliché that some people are in our lives for a "reason, season or a lifetime." So, we need to let go of some people when their season is up. The sooner we understand that fact, the better we can deal with the threats to our identity in this area.

2) <u>Affirmation:</u> If you are shaky about who you are, you may be looking for someone to affirm or validate you. Typically, the need for affirmation is tied to the things you do because that's what your identity is connected to. I used to be a perfectionist, which I got from my mother who was also a perfectionist. If I came home with a report card with all "A's" and an "A-," my mother would say "A-?" In my mind, that meant that I needed to be perfect, which is what began to drive me. It's natural to want our parents or family to pat us on the back when we do well as a child, but the problem arises when we are adults

and still need their affirmation. In the process, those who are looking for affirmation may become people pleasers. They will abandon their own identities to please others.

"For do I now persuade men, or God? or do I seek to please men? for if I yet pleased men, I should not be the servant of Christ."
Galatians 1:10

If you are focused on pleasing man, your service to God will be hindered. You are not alone because I went through this when I was younger. I was so accommodating that it was hard for me to say "no" to those closest to me. The good news is that you can take back what was stolen from you. You can begin to think for yourself, make your own decisions and form your own opinions. Whether we admit it or not, many of us are world class people pleasers. We are held hostage by what others think of us. You may be looking for someone to tell you who you are, but God has already told you. The only escape from what the crowd thinks of you is to discover your "real" identity in Christ.

3) <u>Acceptance:</u> If people have spoken negative things about you, you may be looking for acceptance. Unlike affirmation, acceptance focuses on your perception of yourself rather than what you do. The enemy may be telling you that you are the way you are because...your father was never around, you were molested as a child, nobody ever loved you, you were falsely accused or your parents said you were a failure. You can't give anyone that much power over the direction of your life, which is why your identity needs to be tied to Christ. He is the only One who will love you and

accept you just the way you are, with your issues and all. He loved you before you even loved Him (*1 John 4:19*), which is proof of His total acceptance of you. When your identity is stolen in this area, you will find yourself putting your life or dreams on hold for other people. You will go back to school, start your business, get married, or see the world only after a certain thing or event happens. A woman told me that she couldn't go back to school because she was married and would be turning 55 years old. I asked her how old she would be if she did go back. Do you see my point? I've heard people say that someone makes them feel a certain way, but people don't control what you feel. Your feelings are neutral, so your mind has to tell your emotions what to do. It goes back to your thinking. When you think right, you will feel right.

Attacked by Appearances

Another tactic of the enemy is to attack us about the inadequacies in our appearance. We live in a very vain society, and we are constantly bombarded with commercials on ways to improve our appearance. We have allowed the media to define "beauty" and to dictate how we should look, what we should wear and even what we should eat. There are TV shows like, *The Biggest Loser*, where people lose weight to show off how much better they look. The common message to people is that they don't look good enough, so they need to take steps to fix themselves...like having plastic surgery, tummy tucks or makeovers. We can become so focused on our outer beauty that we often forget about our inner beauty.

After Michael Jackson's death, there was an article in the *Houston Chronicle Outlook* (July 3, 2009) entitled,

"Image in the mirror is what killed Michael." Courtland Milloy, a columnist for the *Washington Post*, started the article with, "What killed Michael Jackson? This autopsy does not require a scalpel. A mirror will do." The article stressed how distortions in self-perception can destroy people and cause them to keep trying to make themselves look better by changing their appearance...their nose, face, eyes or chin. This is the crux of the appearance issue that many of us are also dealing with, and it can negatively impact our self-image.

However, the Bible tells us that we need to take a different approach to our appearance and not worry about fitting into society's idea of beauty. Unlike the world, God doesn't focus on our outward appearance. He is more concerned about what's on the inside. God wants to develop our inner beauty, so that it can be reflected in who we are. Moreover, the outer appearance is not the best way to judge who a person really is. You've heard the saying, "You can't judge a book by its cover," and the same principle applies to people. We have all met people who were nice looking on the outside, but we see a completely different picture once they start talking. These are the type of people who remind us that what is on the outside does not always match what's in the inside.

Why are we so consumed with our looks and appearance then? Unfortunately we do live in a superficial world where people do judge us based on our appearance. If only we could truthfully say that we are not in the majority, and that we all look beyond what's on the outside. However, all of us are influenced by appearances to some degree, but we need to keep looks in the right perspective. While it's okay for you to look nice, you need to avoid going to extremes. It's important that you remain aware of why you do the things you do to look good. Ask yourself two questions: 1) Does the focus on your appearance take your eyes off the Lord? 2) Are you more focused on your weight, clothes or makeup than you are on God? If you answered, "Yes," to either of these questions, then you may need to take a closer look at your priorities. God is more focused on your heart, rather than your appearance.

To lose your identity because of an attack on your appearance is a prevalent form of identity theft. When you look at yourself, you may blame your appearance on your inability to achieve your desires. You may not be in a relationship because you think you are unattractive or overweight. You may think you didn't get that dream job because you are too short, your nose is too big or your legs aren't big enough. When it comes to how you look, there is always something that could be changed. However, you have to learn to love yourself the way you were created.

Sometimes those who have bad things to say about how you look are actually wishing they had your looks. I had a friend who was always teasing me in public about being too small, but one day I got fed up and told her that I was happy with my weight. When I confronted her about her comments, she admitted that she thought she was too fat and wished that she could be my size. Because I knew who I was, I didn't try to change myself to please her or anyone else. Similarly, you can't throw out your spiritual identity because of insecurities related to your appearance. If your identity is tied to how you look, what happens when you gain weight, get gray hair or get scarred from an accident? Do you change into someone else?

POSSESSION TIES

Another way to have our spiritual identities stolen involves trying to fill our void with possessions. These things can only temporarily make us *feel* better about ourselves, but not *make* us better. In effect, we give the enemy the key to steal not only our natural things from us, but more importantly our spiritual identities. No matter how much you have or acquire, you won't find your true identity or fulfillment in your possessions. They are only "things" that you possess, which as you know can be taken from you at anytime. Your car can be repossessed and your house can be foreclosed on, but your true identity should not be affected when it happens. You can't allow the identity thief to rob you of your God-given identity, when it comes to the things and money that you have or don't have. It's not about what you own but who you are.

Tackled by Things

Satan has been busy tackling us with our desire for things while slipping our spiritual identities right out of our pockets at the same time. In effect, he puts the bait out there and easily hooks us when we have visions of grandeur. Society tells us that our status and worth are determined by how many "things" we have acquired. If you can get a bigger house, a new car, a summer home or new furniture, you think that your identity crisis will go away. Well, it won't change anything because things can't satisfy you if your identity is not tied to Christ. The more you have, the more you want. When you are in an identity crisis, you may covet things to fill your void. You may get deeper in debt naturally in an attempt to buy back what's been stolen from you spiritually, but it's not an equivalent replacement. What does it profit a man to gain the whole world and lose his soul?

> "For what is a man profited, if he shall gain the whole world, and lose his own soul? or what shall a man give in exchange for his soul?"
>
> *Matthew 16:26*

The question posed is what does a man benefit if he gains the whole world and everything in it, but loses his soul in the process? The Greek word for "soul" is "psuche", which means inner life. The stakes are high if he gains the entire world, but how does that measure up to him losing himself (who he is on the inside)? In other words, he has all of the natural "things" that he could ever want, but he doesn't know who he is. Not only has he trashed his spiritual identity, but he has also forfeited his spiritual treasures found in Christ. How would you respond to this proposal? What if you could follow the pursuits of this world and have all of the possessions and riches that you want, but lose your soul to the devil? Some people would give up their soul for much less when their identity is tied to their possessions. What could you possibly gain that would be equivalent to the exchange for your soul? Absolutely nothing! You can never put your identity on the hook in order to get more stuff because it won't fill the real void anyway. Only Jesus can do that, so hold on to your soul and your spiritual identity.

Let's look at the parable of the rich young ruler who had to learn the same lesson about his possessions in *Mark 10*. The young man ran up to Jesus and knelt before Him to ask a very serious question, "Good Master, what shall I do that I may inherit eternal life?" (*Mark 10:17*). Jesus initially told him to keep the commandments, which the man quickly confirmed he had observed since his youth. Then, Jesus told him that he lacked one thing, which the man was not ready to hear.

"Then Jesus beholding him loved him, and said unto him, One thing thou lackest: go thy way, sell whatsoever thou hast, and give to the poor, and thou shalt have treasure in heaven: and come, take up the cross, and follow me. And he was sad at that saying, and went away grieved: for he had great possessions."

Mark 10:21-22

Unlike what many of us would do, Jesus got right to the bottom line - the young man's love of the world. Jesus told him to sell his "possessions," give the money away, and follow Him. Yet, the young ruler was unwilling to do this because his worldly possessions were too great. He was more tied to his wealth than he was to Christ. When we embrace Christ, we must let go of the world. The young man was honest with himself because he knew that Christ's standards clashed with his ambitions. He walked away sorrowful because he had "great possessions." What could he possess that had such a hold on him as to make him walk away from eternal life?

In today's terms, I wonder if he had a huge mansion, a fully loaded Bentley, a golf resort in Pebble Beach, a private jet, a Fortune 500 company, a summer home in Beverly Hills or $10 million in the bank. What's the point of having things if you've lost yourself? What happens when your things are lost or stolen? Do you change into someone else?

Mugged by Money

I intentionally dealt with the possessions first because they are only an outgrowth of the bigger issue, money. There is nothing spiritually wrong with money itself, but the problem is with the "love of money." The enemy desires to mug you with money because you need it to buy the possessions that you desire. Then, he uses it to steal your identity. Having or desiring money is not a bad thing by itself, but it's the "love of money" that causes you to lose sight of who you are.

> "For the love of money is the root of all evil: which while some coveted after, they have erred from the faith, and pierced themselves through with many sorrows."
> 1 Timothy 6:10

That love of money is the real stronghold that can easily become an obsession in our lives, especially during tough economic times. We are supposedly in a recession, but I am serving the world notice that I am not participating. I know that my Source is God, and that's where my provision comes from. You must know that the Lord will supply all of your need according to His riches in glory (*Philippians 4:19*). Otherwise, you will look to money as a cure all, but it can never solidify your identity. However, you may think if you had more money, all of your problems would be solved.

> "A feast is made for laughter, and wine maketh merry: but money answereth all things."
> Ecclesiastes 10:19

Here, King Solomon states that money answers "all things." In other words, money is the means by which people obtain everything they want. Money answers the requests of all and supplies them with whatever they need or desire. The expensive feasts were possible because of money. If you understand the principles of stewardship, the more money you have, the more you're responsible for. While money can buy you health insurance, it can't give you health. It can buy you a house, but it can't make it a home. When your identity is in Christ, you should know that it's God who gives you the power to get wealth.

> "But thou shalt remember the LORD thy God: for it is he that giveth thee power to get wealth, that he may establish his covenant which he sware unto thy fathers, as it is this day."
> *Deuteronomy 8:18*

Moses had to remind the Israelites that their provisions came from God, not from their own hands. Sometimes, we also need to be reminded that God is our provider (Jehovah-Jireh) because we can soon forget and think our job is our provision. Like the Israelites, it can be easy for us to forget God when we look at the things that "our" money bought, such as the 401K account, the car, the house, the maid, the chauffeur or the jewelry. Recall how Joseph in the Bible didn't allow his problems or prosperity to cause him to forget God. We don't own the things that God has blessed us with, but we are only His stewards. Without God, you would not be anything or have anything. Have you ever asked yourself, "Why is it that I have more money than I have ever had before and yet I am less content?" If your identity is tied to your money or possessions, what happens when you're broke or have to file bankruptcy? Do you change into someone else?

POSITION TIES

Lastly, we can lose our spiritual identities by connecting them to the positions or titles that we currently hold or desire to hold. People and possessions couldn't change who we are, so why do we think positions and titles are any different? What do you say if someone asks, "Who are you really?" If your reply is, "I am an engineer" or whatever your position is, you're in trouble. That's what you do, but not who you are. What you do doesn't determine who you are. Instead, who you are determines what you do. Your position, career or title can't define who you really are. You may feel like you're now "somebody" because you have a certain position, but it doesn't change who you are. Your titles don't matter – whether you have a Ph.D. or a GED. It's so easy to try to define your identity by business cards, degrees and resumes. Instead, you should be telling people about "you" (your dreams, hopes, purpose, character, and integrity). We can't allow the spiritual identity thief to rob us of our God-given identities in the areas of success and performance.

Socked by Success

Some of us have a proverbial "black eye" because we have allowed the enemy to sock us with success and steal our spiritual identities. We can become so driven by our desire to succeed that we start walking around wondering who we really are. We start looking for various indications of what we think is success, such as our status, position or title, to determine our identity. Climbing the corporate ladder, having a lucrative business, accumulating things and making money are only a mirage for real success. Promotion does not come from the north, south, east or west, but from the Lord.

> "For promotion cometh neither from the east, nor from the west, nor from the south. But God is the judge: he putteth down one, and setteth up another."
>
> *Psalm 75:6-7*

Real success is the continual realization of God's will for your life, not where you work or how much you make.

Your desire for achievements at work or in your business or other associations can rob you of who you really are. Our society has created the standard that our success is quantified by what we do, where we work, where we went to college, etc., which is the polar opposite of God's idea of success. Too often people think that if they receive a certain promotion, reach a certain status or live in a certain area, then they would be happy. Interestingly, once those people have reached that position or location, they still don't have a fulfilling life. When people find out that I am an attorney, I get asked a series of questions: 1) "Where do you work?" 2) "What law school did you go to?" or 3) "How long have you been practicing?" In effect, through these questions, they have summed up my success based on how well I did in their eyes. If I didn't know who I am in Christ, I would have tried to give them all of my "numbers" and statistics to show how successful I am. Some people will even lie, so they can appear more successful than they really are. If you think that you must have the right grades or credentials to get into a prestigious school or a Fortune 500 company, your spiritual identity just got sold to the highest bidder. Remember that "favor" is not fair when it comes to God opening doors for you. I know people who never graduated from high school, but have a lucrative career or business because they know who they are in Christ. You are a child of the Almighty God, and don't you forget it!

Although one of my colleagues professed to a believer and loved his family, he totally indentified himself with his professional success. As a result, when his business took a turn for the worse, he lost his identity and confidence in himself. Similarly, many people are successful by the world's standards, but they are spiritually empty. As believers, the good thing is that we can identify with God. Everything we do should be unto God and not unto man.

> "And whatsoever ye do, do it heartily, as to the Lord, and not unto men;"
>
> *Colossians 3:23*

When you make God the focus of whatever you do, you can stay connected to your spiritual identity. Can you lose your identity when it's tied to Him? No, it's the most solid identity that you can ever have because it is attached to God Himself. If you identify yourself with God, you should know that you are important because God created you. However, if your identity is tied to your success, what happens when you are fired or laid off from your job or have to retire? Do you change into someone else?

Punched by Performance

Check your body for bruises because the enemy has also punched some of us by telling us that high performance equals success. We have bought into the misconception that the harder we work, the more we will be recognized for our performance. I can tell you that's not always the case. In fact, those who "act" like they're working hard while playing the company politics seem more often to receive recognition. The hard workers are usually taken for granted because they do their job without complaining. Some people are deluded into thinking that if they stay busy enough and keep a fast pace, then they will have success. Yet all they find is stress, ulcers, and heart attacks. Eventually, workaholics learn that the satisfaction of doing a good job is short-lived. I am not telling you what I've heard, but what I know.

The sports arena is a good example of how a person's performance can become the measurement of their success. When this happens, they are allowing their real identity to be stolen while they are dunking on the basketball court or making a touchdown on the field. The trouble for many athletes, even believers, is that their sport often takes the place of Christ when it comes to their identities. They may be a Christian and seeking Him off the court, but it is their sport that truly defines who they are. They are an athlete first, and a believer second. Their lives are consumed by stats and scoreboards. It may not be intentional, but they may have a hard time giving Christ first place in their lives. Why are they so susceptible to this way of living? Since sports are performance based games, the high performers get the TV commercials and the big contracts.

The performance issue is not limited to the work arena, but has also spilled over into the church and other areas. I was raised in church all my life and got saved at an early age. I knew God, but I didn't have a close personal relationship with Him until later. We were taught that we had to "work" out our soul salvation. Some people took that literally. They started to think that their salvation was based on what they did or did not do. They were constantly trying to get involved in as many activities in church as proof of their relationship with God. They were in the choir, teaching Bible study, on the deacon's board or in the women's or men's ministry. However, as you know, we were saved by grace through faith and not by works. When you become performance based, it will eventually spill over into every area of your life. If your identity is tied to your performance and how well you do, then you could lose your identity if you fail at a task or don't do as well as expected. What happens if you get a bad evaluation or fail at an assignment at work? Do you change into someone else? Hopefully, each time this question was asked at the end of the discussion of each of the 3 P's, your answer was "no."

The 3 P's are some of the key spiritual identity thieves in our lives. In order to rob you of who you are, these thieves will lie to you by saying things, like "you are...": a) not smart or educated enough, b) not good enough, c) not attractive enough, d) not rich enough or e) not born in the right family or with the right pedigree. However, you can't buy into those lies, but instead go back to what God says about you. Now that you have identified the sources of your spiritual identity, it's time to target the real enemy.

TABLE 3
The 3P's Connected To Your Stolen Identity

3P's	TIE NO. 1	TIE NO. 2
PEOPLE TIES	**Robbed by <u>Relationships</u>** • Need for affection • Need for affirmation • Need for acceptance	**Attacked by <u>Appearances</u>** • Concern about looks • Concern about image • Concern about size
POSSESSION TIES	**Tackled by <u>Things</u>** • Focus on world • Focus on wealth • Focus on lifestyle	**Mugged by <u>Money</u>** • Obsessed with money • Obsessed with power • Obsessed with credit
POSITION TIES	**Socked by <u>Success</u>** • Key is what you do • Key is what you have • Key is who you know	**Punched by <u>Performance</u>** • Seeks recognition • Seeks promotion • Seeks advancement

Chapter 9

Target The Real Enemy

Now that you have conducted a thorough search of the sources of your stolen identity, you should know exactly what's been stolen and how it was stolen from you. During the process, your focus should have been mainly on your own actions, those that could have played a role in your identity being snatched. So, the next logical target is the "enemy," who actually stole your identity and turned your life upside down. The term, "enemy" refers to someone who hates you or wishes to harm you, which is typically the motive for identity theft. In the natural, the enemy (the imposter) desires to harm you and usually follows through when he or she steals your money, credit and peace of mind.

As soon as you find out about the identity theft, your initial reaction is to want to see the enemy pay for what he or she has done to you. When I realized that the police were not aggressively going after the thief who stole my identity, I had to put a face on this "faceless" enemy. As a result, I had to find out everything I could about the identity of the perpetrator to fully uncover all of the damage that she had done to me. After months of intensive searching, I was able to identify the thief and turn over all of the evidence against her to the police. However, she ended up getting a slap on the wrist for all the trouble that she caused me. I was furious because once I knew who the enemy was, she became my target. Likewise, when it comes to the theft of our spiritual identities, we have to identify and target the "real enemy." We have to find out everything we can about the invisible "enemy" that is out to steal our spiritual identities. However, we don't have to be concerned about whether this enemy will have to pay because he definitely will.

The "Devil" You Know

We've all heard the expression, "it's better to deal with the devil you know." The saying means that it's often better to deal with someone or something that you are familiar with, even if it's not ideal, than take a risk with an unknown person or thing. I have heard people use this cliché when they are having problems on their jobs or in their marriages, but they are not willing to make a change in those areas. They would rather stay in their current miserable situation than to take a chance on something different. Many of us take the same approach when it comes to our identities, preferring to deal with the devil that we know.

As stated in Chapter 3, many of us are watching out for the random strangers rather than the people we know when it comes to identity theft. However, according to the FTC in 2000, 19% of all victims of identity theft had a personal relationship with the thief, and 10% of those thieves were family members. That's a frightening statistic because we are trying to protect ourselves from strangers, when we should be more concerned about the people that we know. How many people do you know who would be able to answer basic security questions asked by your creditors? You know the questions like, "What's your mother's maiden name?" or "What is your date of birth?" I don't mention this to make you paranoid, but to raise your awareness of the type of crime you're dealing with. In fact, many thefts occur because a close friend or relative who is having financial problems steals your information, so he or she can get a cell phone, a car, a house or a computer or open a bank account. This is exactly what happened to me. Desperate thieves will steal from their friends, their relatives or even their own children. Not only will they steal your personal information to use your credit, but also for employment, insurance, benefits and social security fraud. This is why it's so important that you know who the enemy is and how he or she operates.

If you personally know the enemy who stole your identity, you may feel more betrayed, especially if it was a friend or relative. However, you may find it difficult to turn the person in to the police. After the charges were filed against my cousin for stealing my identity, the prosecutor contacted me to confirm if I wanted to pursue the charges since it involved a relative. I told her, "Absolutely!" With identity theft, you have to file charges against the thief to get the financial burden of the fraudulent accounts off of you and to clear your name, so I didn't have a choice. If the enemy is willing to do the crime, then she has to be willing to do the time. The prosecutor also asked me if I would be okay if the thief received felony probation. While my flesh wanted to say throw the book at her and give her the maximum sentence, I told the prosecutor that I only wanted to see justice done. However, I was outraged when I found out that the thief pled guilty and the felony charges were dropped to a misdemeanor. Nevertheless, my name was cleared, and I was not ultimately held liable for any of the fraudulent accounts or the mortgage loan after years of fighting them.

If the imposter who stole your identity is an unknown stranger, you may feel afraid and constantly wonder if the person standing next to you at the store or walking past you on the street is the enemy. You may distrust everyone, but it's important to focus on the crime not the criminal. You may want the criminal to be brought to justice, but the reality is that it may not occur or the sentence may not be in proportion to the damage done to you. As a result, the primary goal in going after the thief is to make sure that you get your stolen identity back, both naturally and spiritually.

One of my favorite TV shows, *Criminal Minds*, is about a team of FBI profilers who fly to the location of criminal activity to profile various serial killers. It differs from other crime shows because the focus is on the *criminal* rather than the *crime* itself. The tagline for the show is "To stay one step ahead of a criminal takes a criminal mind." In other words, to understand how a criminal operates, you have to think like he or she does. That's the whole purpose of doing a profile on the criminal, which is essential to ensure that you target the real enemy.

After my natural identity theft, I had to do a "profile" on the thief who stole my identity. I was able to figure out who she was by gathering information about her and what she had done in the past. Each credit report and fraudulent credit application with her name on it brought me closer to finding the enemy. She had been a petty criminal, shoplifter and thief for years, but her dirty work had finally caught up with her.

As we get ready to profile the "real" enemy (Satan) who is out to steal our spiritual identities, we must keep in mind that our battle is not natural, but spiritual.

> "For we wrestle not against flesh and blood, but against principalities, against powers, against the rulers of the darkness of this world, against spiritual wickedness in high places."
>
> *Ephesians 6:12*

This scripture emphasizes that our battle is not with people, but the invisible forces that are at work against us. Since we don't see what the enemy is doing in the spiritual world with our natural eyes, it's so easy to try to target the people who we can see. However, the evil forces behind the scenes in this world are our real opposition. You know the old cliché, "You can't bring a knife to a gun fight." We have to understand the type of battle we're in, so we can bring the right weapon to the fight. Our weapons are not carnal, but mighty through God (2 Corinthians 10:4). Moreover, we have to put on the "whole armor of God," so that we will be able to stand against the wiles of the devil. Our "spiritual armor" includes: our belt of truth, breastplate of righteousness, preparation of the gospel of peace, shield of faith, helmet of salvation, and sword of the spirit, which is the Word of God (*Ephesians 6:14-17*).

It's "natural" for us to want to go after the people who have been used by the enemy as the stealing forces in our lives. However, your spouse, coworker or hater, who has done you wrong is not your "real" enemy, even though they may be used by the enemy. They are just puppets, but the enemy is the puppet master that's pulling their strings. In turn, you can't solely focus on who stole your identity, but rather on what you need to do to get it back. The main purpose of this book is to help you target the real enemy because that's who you're actually fighting against. I call him "the devil that you do know."

Once we recognize that our spiritual identities have been stolen with the help of those closest to us, it's not uncommon for us to become bitter and refuse to forgive the "people" whom we see as our enemy. Before you can move forward, you have to know that the real enemy has done this to you.

> "He said unto them, An enemy hath done this. The servants said unto him, Wilt thou then that we go and gather them up?"
>
> *Matthew 13:28*

After Jesus had told the parable of the sower, He spoke this parable of the wheat and the tares with a different twist. His point was that after a farmer had sown his wheat seed, an "enemy" came at night to sow weeds in the same soil. As a result, the wheat and the weeds began to grow together and would continue until harvest time. If the farmer tried to separate the weeds early, then the wheat would be destroyed. The farmer had not done anything wrong to cause this problem, so he needed to know that the enemy (Satan) had done it. In the same manner, we must recognize that a lot of the weeds of destruction that have been growing in our hearts and minds were sown by the enemy.

Before we can go into our spiritual battle, we need to be familiar with who the real enemy is and how his criminal mind works. We need to know where he came from and why he's so determined to steal our spiritual identities. The enemy goes by different names, but his original name was "Lucifer" (the son of the morning) (*Isaiah 14:12*). He started out as one of the chief angels created by God until he rebelled against God and was thrown out of heaven. Then, his name changed to "Satan," which is the Hebrew word meaning "to oppose" or "adversary," which is what he does to us as believers. He is also known by the name, "Devil," which is the Greek word for "to slander." He also has many other aliases, such as the "prince of darkness," "the prince of this world," "the old serpent," "the tempter," "the adversary," "the antichrist," "the father of lies," and "the evil one." Satan has also been referred to as a "wolf in sheep's clothing" (*Matthew 7:15*) because he hides himself just like the identity thief. We may know his many names, but we need to understand his games.

The Tricks Of The Trade

Satan uses many schemes to try to steal from us. If he just gets enough access to our spiritual identities, he has an "open door" to make us question who we are. In turn, we can easily hand over our identities to him. However, don't be fooled, he has still "stolen" it even if we were tricked out of it. That's why we need to know the tricks of his trade.

In *Ephesians 6:11*, Paul explicitly tells us how the devil operates. He states, "Put on the whole armour of God, that ye may be able to stand against the *wiles* of the devil." In order to protect our identities, we need to understand "the wiles of the devil." The word "wiles" is taken from the word "methodos," which literally means "with a road" and is where we get the English word "method." In effect, the enemy is on a road of destruction and has a method (strategy) to get us to join him. He doesn't come out announcing who he is or wearing a red suit with a tail and holding a pitchfork because he's a pickpocket. At times, he actually disguises himself by transforming into an angel of light (2 Corinthians 11:14). Since Satan uses crafty tricks with the intent to deceive us, we have to arm ourselves with the knowledge of his many methods.

It's time for us to focus on the specific "wiles" of the enemy, so we will not naively take the road that he has laid out for us. His strategy is to get us to go in a direction away from God, so he can steal or help us lose our spiritual identities. Satan's names give us a good description of who he is as well as insight into his many games. Let's take a closer look at the following names, which describe the tactics that he uses against us:

a) Liar (*John 8:44* – father of lies): Satan's favorite weapon is lying. He lies to try to damage your relationship with God and others. He (the serpent) lied to Eve in the Garden of Eden when he tricked her into eating the forbidden fruit and will also try to lie to you. Since he is the father of lies, that's all he knows how to do is lie. All I can say is, "The devil is a liar!"

b) Accuser (*Revelation 12:10* – accuser of the brethren): He seeks to accuse God's children before Him day and night, but we overcome him by the blood of the Lamb and by the word of our testimony (*Revelation 12:11*). When Satan tries to accuse you before God of your past mistakes,

remember that you have an Advocate (Jesus Christ) in heaven who defends you against Satan's accusations.
c) <u>Deceiver</u> (*Revelation 12:9* – old serpent, devil, Satan deceived the whole world): He attempts to deceive you so that you will live in sin. When you are deceived, you will believe a lie over the truth, which is what he desires.
d) <u>Adversary</u> (*1 Peter 5:8* – your adversary the devil): The legal term, "adversary," refers to the one opposed to you in a lawsuit, which is the same thing the enemy does in our lives. He wants to destroy you and oppose all that is good in your life because he is your adversary.

This is not an exhaustive list, but only a few tricks that the enemy uses to try to get his hands on our identities. He hopes that we will be careless and let our guards down, so he can sneak in to do his damage.

Our real enemy (Satan) is a thief, and he will rob you of your mind, gifts, talents, finances, family and your very essence if he can. That's why we can't play with the devil because he doesn't play fair. In fact, he is not playing at all, but is in it to win your soul in hell. When God gives you a "word," the enemy comes along to steal it because it's the most powerful tool that you have, and once it penetrates your heart, your eyes are open to who you really are.

When the enemy steals your identity, you do things like lying, stealing, fornicating, committing adultery or just settling for less in life, letting people run over you or never speaking up for yourself. Maybe you don't love yourself, you overeat because you're unhappy or you think everyone is better off than you. Don't believe the thief who stole from you. Once Satan steals who you really are, he gives you a "false" identity and now you're walking around trying to be someone you're not.

Now let's look at a very important truth in spiritual warfare. Paul tells us that we are the determining factor in whether the devil can operate in our lives. He says, "Neither give place to the devil" (*Ephesians 4:27*). If he has a place, that means we gave it to him. The Amplified Bible says, "Leave no room or foothold for the devil…give no opportunity to him." When we allow openings in our spiritual lives, the devil feels like he has the right to take advantage of us. If we keep the doors closed, he can't do what he wants to do in our lives. That's why it is so important that we recognize and close any "open doors" in our lives where the enemy can get in.

One possible open door for the enemy is through generational curses (*Exodus 20:5*) that have attached to our families. We can still be affected today by the things that our ancestors did in the past that we are unaware of. Another open door for the enemy is when we experience an emotionally, challenging situation, which we try to suppress and don't want to deal with. At some point, it's going to come back again, and it may be more difficult to address the longer we wait. As a result, you must identify any open doors for the enemy to get into your life and go back and close them. Otherwise, the enemy will continue to come in and out of the doors, which will keep you in the midst of a spiritual identity crisis. You can't bury your head in the sand and expect the enemy to go away voluntarily, especially if you have opened the door for him. He will take it as a standing invitation to come to your spiritual house and make himself at home like an unwelcomed guest.

Satan is not just an identity thief, but the "enemy of the Kingdom." He wants to infiltrate the lives of every believer that he can tap into, which is a crime against God's kingdom. He is similar to what we call an "enemy of the state," which is a person accused of certain crimes against the state, such as treason. For example, a double agent who sells military secrets that undermine the nation's security would be considered an enemy (not of just one person), but the entire state. I recall a movie, *Enemy of the State*, which sheds some light on how the enemy works. In the movie, the government tried to frame the star, Robert Clayton Dean, for the murder of a U.S. senator led by the corrupt National Security Agency official, Thomas Reynolds. Dean was a devoted father, husband, and attorney shopping for a gift for his wife, and his friend slipped a videotape of the murder into his bag. The real "enemy of the state," Reynolds, was able to take over Dean's life without him knowing and had transmitters all over him – in his watch, pants and shoes – so he could track his every move. Since Dean wasn't up to date on the high-tech gadgets, he didn't understand the wiles of his enemy. As a result, he opened the door for his enemy to steal his "identity." He later teamed up with an ex-intelligence operative, Brill, who schooled him on the tricks of the trade. Although his life was a disaster, Dean decided to fight to get his identity and family back. Just like Dean, many of us have given the "enemy of the Kingdom" access to our lives, and it's up to us to shut him down and take our identities back.

The tools that we use to protect our natural identities are not effective in guarding against spiritual identity theft. However, there are steps that we can take to protect our spiritual identity, and we will explore those options. Let's address the following four important tools to thwart the enemy's attempts to steal our identities.

1) **Be aware of who he is**
   The first tool is to be aware of who your real enemy is and how he works. The more aware and up to date you are on Satan, the better prepared you are to stop his attacks and to act quickly if he does. In order to get the 411 on the devil, you have to go to the Word of God.

2) **Be watchful of his tricks**
   The second tool is to be watchful of the tricks of the enemy and understand how he operates. You can't sleep on the job when it comes to Satan, but you have to keep watch and stay alert at all times (1 Thessalonians 5:6). You have to continually keep your spiritual eyes open and know what the enemy is up to, so he will not be able to sneak into your life.

3) **Be proactive against him**
   The third tool is to be proactive against your adversary (Satan). Just being aware of his tricks is useless unless you take steps to address his threats. You have to be sober and vigilant against him because he goes around looking for people to devour (1 Peter 5:8). You have to be ready to go after him before he tries to come after you.

4) **Be familiar with where he goes**
   The fourth tool is to be familiar with where the enemy goes to look for his prey. You can't allow the enemy to lead you down the wrong road or catch you in places where you shouldn't be. Satan tries to allure you to places where you are more susceptible to him, like casinos, bars or strip clubs. If that's a place where you're vulnerable, you are giving him an open door. Instead you must stay where you know you are safe (in God's will).

I call these tools the "Be-attitudes" of spiritual identity theft protection. When it comes to safeguarding your spiritual identity, you need to change your attitude and take the necessary precautions to stay a step ahead of the enemy.

Let's be clear that we can't assume or give credit to Satan for everything that goes wrong in our lives. While, he is usually behind a lot of it, we can't blame it all on him. We need to know that he exists and how he attacks us, but we shouldn't constantly dwell on it. Many of us are so spiritual that we are no earthly good. We need balance even when we deal with the real enemy. We need to know what he is capable of, but must not forget that we have the Lord on our side. There are many biblical examples of believers who refused to dwell on Satan's intervention in their lives or work, like Joshua, Nehemiah, Esther and Daniel. Because they knew who God created them to be, they didn't give in to the threats and distractions of their enemy. While we do have a real enemy, we are not defenseless. We have to keep our focus on God, no matter what tricks Satan throws our way. On another note, don't forget to watch out for the enemy called "me" because we can be our worse enemy. Sometimes, we can be harder on ourselves and do more damage to our identities than Satan ever could.

The Faceoff

Once you know who the real enemy is, you have to be prepared for a faceoff to get your stolen identity back. A "faceoff" simply means a confrontation, which typically involves a showdown between two opponents. Identity theft is considered a "faceless" crime because the thief doesn't show his or her face when he or she steals from you, and this makes proving the crime very difficult for the victim. In my identity theft case, I had to put a face on the imposter. Since she was applying for credit cards on her "new" computer -- fraudulently purchased with my identity -- it was not enough that I had obtained the applications with her personal information and signature. Once she applied for credit and was approved online, she would get an email confirmation that informed her to come into the store to sign the application. At that time, she was required to provide proof of her identity and sign the application. Since she was using her own name with my social security number at that time, she was able to prove her identity to the retailers.

However, the prosecutor could only charge her with one count of identity theft because only one store could identify her "face" in a photo spread. Although the thief later confessed the crime to me, she told the police that her driver's license had been stolen and that she didn't know anything about the theft. Without putting her face with the other counts of identity theft, there was not enough evidence to prosecute her. Ironically, when I came face-to-face with the thief, she had the nerve to tell me, "The devil made me do it." That was one time she actually told the truth.

Before we can even have a faceoff with the real enemy, we have to get him to show his face. When I finally joined Facebook, I was surprised at the number of people who didn't have a "face" on their profiles. I was a little confused that a face was not required on "Facebook." These faceless people will send me a friend invite with a silhouette of a face, so I don't even know who they are. I don't accept any friends without a face. You have to show your face if you want to come into my circle. Likewise, we can't let suspected enemies into our lives until we can see their face, so at least they won't be able to sneak in. If the enemy does get in, at least we should make an informed decision about whether to open the door for him.

The faceoff that we often have with the enemy reminds me of the movie, *Faceoff,* about FBI agent, Sean Archer, who had been trying to apprehend a terrorist who was his arch enemy, Castor Troy. Archer had hunted Troy for eight years to get revenge for the death of his son. To do this, Archer had to "borrow" Troy's face and assume his identity to go undercover as Troy, but things went wrong when Troy woke up from a coma and assumed Archer's identity and face. Eventually, the two men had a "faceoff," and it was not pretty.

Archer's wife had to identify her "real" husband from who he was on the inside, regardless of the fact that his face didn't match his words. Archer was able to eventually bring Troy down and get his face back, but it required a faceoff to do it. Although the face switch was a little far-fetched, that is what Satan does from a spiritual perspective – steal your face (identity). Likewise, you will eventually have a faceoff with the enemy if you want to get your "face" and identity back. Remember that when Satan steals your identity, he doesn't want to be like you, but instead wants you to be like him. After you have a faceoff with the real enemy, you are on the path to the full recovery of your stolen identity.

STEP 3
Review Questions

1) Is your spiritual identity totally tied to the only "reliable" Source, God? If not, what is it tied to (e.g., a relationship, position, job, etc.)? Which ties do you need to let go of? Why?

2) What does it mean to be "in Christ" (*2 Corinthians 5:17*)? How does it apply in your daily life? What are some of the personal benefits that you have received by identifying with Christ?

3) What does it mean that Jesus came to give us "life...more abundantly" in *John 10:10*? Do you think He was talking about physical prosperity, spiritual life eternally or both? Have you embraced the abundant life? If not, why?

4) Have you allowed the enemy to pick your pockets and steal your spiritual identity? Did you do a personal inventory to confirm exactly what was missing in your life? Were you already aware of it?

5) Is your spiritual identity vulnerable in the three key areas of Satan's attack: people, possessions, and positions (3 P's)? If so, in what areas do you need to make changes (be specific)?

6) When your spiritual identity was stolen, did you target the real enemy, Satan? Or did you go after or blame the people that he used? Are you familiar with the "wiles" of the enemy? If so, has it helped you in your fight against him?

STEP 4

INITIATE
The Full Recovery

"And David inquired at the LORD, saying, Shall I pursue after this troop? shall I overtake them? And he answered him, Pursue: for thou shalt surely overtake them, and without fail **recover all**."

1 Samuel 30:8

POETIC EXHORTATION
The Full Recovery

You have to initiate your full recovery,

Now that you've done your self-discovery,

All that was missing you should finally see,

So snatch it all back from the "real" enemy,

For only then will you be completely free,

To rightfully reclaim your "stolen" identity.

STEP 4
Overview

The fourth step in the process of recovering your stolen identity is to <u>initiate</u> the full recovery. Now that you know exactly what's missing, how it was taken and who stole it from you, the last step is to recover everything that you've lost. You have to "initiate" the recovery process because no one (definitely not the thief) is going to do it for you. All you have to do is take the first step, and the Lord will walk through it with you. When I found out that my natural identity had been stolen, I had to initiate the process of recovering my identity. If I had waited for the police, the creditors, the federal agencies or even my family to take action, I would still be waiting. Since it was "my stuff" that was taken, I was the only one truly concerned about getting it back. Since I had the burden to prove my innocence, I had an incentive to start the process right away to clear my name.

After I began my recovery process for the natural theft, I had to do all of the work. I had to gather all of the facts and order copies of my credit reports before I could even report the crime to the police, my creditors and the FTC. It was a long and grueling process for me to "fully" recover my identity. However, I was persistent in getting it all back, so I didn't have to pay any of the fraudulent credit card bills or the mortgage loan and was able to restore my good credit. In fact, my credit score actually ended up being higher after the identity theft than it had been before it happened. That's what I call a "full recovery," where I end up in a better position than when I first started. Additionally, I was able to get my stuff back because I knew exactly what was missing. When it comes to our spiritual identities, we also need to know what belongs to us in order to have a full recovery of everything that we've lost.

REFLECTIONS ON
Identity Theft

"Cleaning up after ID [theft] is a marathon, not a sprint. Prepare your mind accordingly."

Frank Mellot
Identity Theft Resource Center

"A professional thief can assume your identity in just a few hours, but it can take years for you to restore your credit standing and identity."

Identity Theft Shield

Chapter 10

On The Road To Recovery

It may feel like a long time coming, but you are finally on the road to recovery of your stolen identity. I know first-hand that it is not an easy process to get to this point, but you have made it. You're almost to the finish line, so it's too late to turn back now. If you knew what you had to go *through* to get your identity back, you probably would have thrown in the towel a long time ago. However, you chose to keep moving forward despite your fears, your frustrations, your failures and all of the losses related to the theft of your spiritual identity. You can start rejoicing now because not only are you about to get your stolen identity back, but you will also finally discover who you really are in Christ. To do so, you need to know what you're actually entitled to recover. Otherwise, you may end up with only a "partial" recovery instead of a "full" one. When your identity was initially stolen, you ended up on a road of self-doubt where you were constantly searching for meaning, seeking approval from others and trying to prove that you are valuable. However, now you're on a very different road, the road to recovery of your real identity.

Know What You're Entitled To

Before you can even initiate your recovery process from a natural perspective, you need to be clear on what the applicable law says you're entitled to recover. If there is no law, there can't be a crime. Initially, thieves were getting away with identity theft because there was no law. Even after it became a law, additional steps were needed to help with the enforcement of the law. What good is a law if the criminals can't be prosecuted under it?

When my natural identity was stolen, I didn't know any specifics about the identity theft law. Not until I started doing research did I become familiar with it. I was shocked to find out that before 1998, identity theft didn't even have a name. The technology and methods used by thieves to steal the identity of innocent victims were more advanced than the laws. I was curious about what actually prompted the enactment of the law, which was quite interesting. In one infamous case of identity theft, it was unbelievable what the criminal, who was a convicted felon, did to his unsuspecting victim. He incurred more than $100,000 of credit card debt, obtained a federal home loan, and bought homes, motorcycles and handguns in the victim's name. In fact, he called his victim to taunt him before filing for bankruptcy in the victim's name and told him that he could continue to pose as the victim for as long as he wanted because identity theft was not a crime. While the victim and his wife spent more than four years and more than $15,000 of their own money to restore their credit, the criminal served a brief sentence for making a false statement to procure a firearm, but he made no restitution to his victim for all of the harm he had caused. Sadly, sometimes the thieves know more about the law than we do. This case, and others like it, prompted the U.S. Congress to create a new federal offense of identity theft.

The more you know about the law that is intended to protect your "identity," the more equipped you will be to initiate your recovery. Once I knew the identity theft law, I was able to start the process to get my identity back. In my case, the thief's sentence was dropped from a felony to a misdemeanor with a reduced sentence of six days, of which she only served three days. The identity thief in my case actually served more time for shoplifting than she did for stealing my identity. Since I was not informed when she decided to plead guilty, I didn't get a chance to request or receive any restitution from her. When I found out, I was very upset. The prosecutor later informed me that she didn't have a strong case, which is why she pushed for a plea. It was obvious to me that the District Attorney's Office was not serious about prosecuting this faceless crime until later after the District Attorney's identity was stolen.

Generally, the court can order a thief to pay a certain amount of money as restitution to the victim of identity theft to reimburse him or her for his or her losses. While some judges are reluctant to order restitution, they are required to listen to your request and will usually consider reasonable costs that you incurred to investigate your case. You would need to write a letter to the judge requesting restitution with the following details about the impact to you (financially, emotionally and physically) and your actual losses. Then, the judge would make the decision on how much restitution you would be entitled to. Some identity theft victims eventually recover from the crime, but many victims don't. This assumes that the thief is even caught or has any money, but it doesn't mean that the victim will automatically recover anything.

Unfortunately, the natural laws don't always guarantee justice for identity theft victims, but it is good to know that God does. As the "victim" of spiritual identity theft, you are entitled to a "full recovery" of everything that the enemy took from you. Once the Supreme Judge (God) rules in your favor, the invisible thief is obligated to pay you a full restitution. The word, "restitution," means to return to the rightful owner whatever was taken away. In other words, it's time for you to get your "full" identity back.

When it comes to spiritual identity theft, you don't have to worry about getting payback against Satan. Your job is to inventory your actual losses from the spiritual crime, and then you can turn the case over to the Judge (God). He will make sure that Satan is indicted, which means formally charged, for the crime he has committed against you (see Table 4). In turn, the Lord will handle the conviction and punishment for the enemy.

> "...Vengeance is mine; I will repay, saith the Lord."
> *Romans 12:19*

In this scripture, Paul reaffirms that we should leave vengeance against those who harmed us to the Lord, whether it's Satan or the people that he used. Unlike the natural crime, we can rest assured that God's payback on our behalf will be in proportion to the crime. When my identity was stolen, a friend told me that I should pull the thief out into the street and beat her like she stole something (which she did). Despite how upset I was, I had to release it to God. Although she only served three days in jail, I knew God's justice would be served in the long run. I had to "Let go and let God!" Only after I got to that point was I able to receive peace and obtain my full recovery.

Just like the identity thief has to pay restitution for the natural crime, the same holds true in the spiritual realm. The enemy of our soul, Satan, has to pay up when he tries to steal our spiritual identities. He is determined to do everything in his power to break the 8th commandment in the Bible, "Thou shalt not steal" (*Exodus 20:15*), which is his key goal for our identities. The Bible also provides some guidance on what a victim of theft is entitled to from a thief:

> "Men do not despise a thief, if he steal to satisfy his soul when he is hungry; But if he be found, he shall restore sevenhold; he shall give all the substance of his house."
>
> *Proverbs 6:30-31*

The penalty for a thief who stole because he was hungry was not as severe as stealing based on greed. However, any kind of stealing was considered wrong and was punishable. Moreover, if the thief was found, he had to restore seven times more than he stole to his victim. I hope Satan is ready to pay up because once we add up our losses; he can multiply them by seven to figure out what he owes us.

The Burden Is On You

If your natural identity is stolen, you will have the burden of proving that you are actually a "victim." A "victim" refers to the person who suffers loss as a result of someone else's action. Unlike victims of violent crimes, such as robbery, assault or rape, who are generally treated with respect and sympathy, identity theft victims are often treated as if they are the criminals. Identity theft victims often find themselves having to prove that they're "victims" instead of deadbeats who are trying to avoid paying bad debts. Identity theft is considered a "victimless" crime, so it is low on the priority list for the police. Since the victims don't have visible scars, the police and courts may think they have not really been harmed. I felt as if I was presumed guilty until I could prove that I was innocent. What happened to "innocent until proven guilty?" How do you go about proving something you didn't do? I had to prove a negative...I didn't make any of the fraudulent charges or enter into the mortgage loan. The key to surviving the process was to get the right documents and to send them to the right people to prove my innocence. The fraudulent applications and documents may help to prove that you are a victim and contain valuable information about the thief. I was told several times that I needed to seek legal advice, so I had to provide my own legal services since I was the only attorney willing to take my case on a pro bono basis.

Most cases of identity theft involve at least two victims: 1) the individual whose personal information is used to commit crimes, and 2) the company that granted the credit or loan. Generally, the individual will typically be off the hook for any financial liability *if* he or she can prove that he or she is a victim, which is not always easy to do. However, the creditors are often left holding the loss, but they often refuse to file charges against the thief because of the time and expense involved. If you don't even report the crime, you definitely will not be entitled to any restitution.

During my recovery process, I had to spend more than 75% of my time proving that I was a "victim." I thought I would at least get the benefit of the doubt from the creditors, but that was not the case since they were focused on minimizing their losses. I had to keep retelling my story to prove my "victim" status, which was very frustrating because the entire burden was on me. I had to go to four different police departments just to file a police report.

Since the police report was a critical document for proving that I was a victim, I had to run all over town to get one. I had to provide it, along with my ID theft affidavit, to the credit bureaus and my creditors. In addition, the mortgage company also required me to do a forgery affidavit. In fact, they informed me that the guard at the gate of the house that was fraudulently purchased in my name said, "DeMonica Gladney lives here." I could not believe that I had to prove that I was not living in two houses in two different states at the same time. Not only was I overwhelmed by the whole process, I felt stonewalled by the very people I turned to for help. Identity theft is a difficult crime to prove, and I quickly learned that the wheels of justice turn very slowly. Despite all of the odds that appeared to be against me, I would not have been able to recover from the crime if I had not reported or pursued it.

When it came to the theft of my spiritual identity, I later realized that I was also spending most of my time trying to prove that I was a "victim." After I discovered the spiritual crime, I felt compelled to tell everyone I believed to be involved in the crime what had been stolen from me spiritually and how they had contributed to my problems. What I had not realized was that I had a "presumption of innocence" because I was covered by the blood of Jesus, so I didn't have to prove anything. All I needed to do was to contact the Supreme Judge, God, who already had all of the proof related to my case. Unlike the natural crime, I didn't need to call the police, the creditors or the credit bureaus to prove anything. However, for the spiritual theft, you still need to know the right people to tell about your crime. As the victim, you may be eager to confront every "identity thief" who you think had any involvement in stealing your spiritual identity. You may go tell your parents, your ex-spouse or your children, and of course they don't even think you're a victim. As a result, you may find yourself trying to prove that you are. However, they are not the right people to be talking to because only God can give you a full recovery from the spiritual crime. You wouldn't call Dell if you have a problem with your Sony laptop. After you read the manufacturer's instructions, then you would call the company that made the computer. Likewise, the Bible is the instruction manual for believers. If there's a problem with your spiritual identity, you have to go to the Creator (God) who gave it to you. He made you, so He is the only one who knows who you are supposed to be and how you're supposed to function.

Even when you are in the process of recovering your spiritual identity, Satan will try to make you prove who you are. He wants to treat you like a "victim," so you will continue to try to justify who God created you to be. Once you have turned the crime over to God, there is nothing else for you to prove to the enemy or anyone else. Satan tried this same trick with Jesus, but it didn't work. As discussed earlier, He tried to get Jesus to prove who He was in the wilderness. When he tempted Jesus by saying, "If you be the son of God...," Jesus responded, "And it is written..." Jesus knew who He was, so He didn't need to prove anything to the devil. In fact, He sent Him to the Word as the only proof. Likewise, when Satan comes your way asking for proof of your spiritual identity, you need to send him to the Word and let him figure it out. The critical point is that once you're on the road to recovery of your stolen identity, you are no longer a "victim" and should not act like one.

No Longer The "Victim"

When I was trying to find resources to help me with my natural identity theft, I ran across a step-by-step guide on the subject, *From Victim to Victor: A Step-By-Step Guide For Ending The Nightmare of Identity Theft*, by Mari Frank, a nationally recognized identity theft expert. It is an amazing and thorough resource with all the tools you need to recover from identity theft. The author is an attorney who was also a "victim" of identity theft and had to figure out how to survive the legal maze. After reading the book, it dawned on me that I was still calling myself a "victim" while I was in my recovery phase. I had been so consumed with proving that I was a victim, that I had, in fact, started acting like one. In my mind, a victim is someone who is helpless and looking for someone else to resolve his or her problem. If I was going to make it through this tedious process, I had to realize that I was no longer a victim. I was on the road to recovery, so I was now a "victor" even before I received my full recovery. When I knew that I was not in this fight alone, I started thinking like a victor. For all of the companies who were treating me like the criminal, I had to change my way of thinking. Rather than looking to them to help me resolve the identity theft, I had to use the legal and spiritual knowledge that I had to do it myself. To the same companies that were sending me letters demanding payment for the fraudulent debts, I started sending demand letters, ordering them to remove the debts from my credit report. I had to move mentally, emotionally, physically and legally from a "victim" to a "victor."

Once I let go of my victim mentality, I realized that I had to believe the Truth (the Word) and not just rely on the facts. Based on the facts, I should not have been able to recover from the impact of the identity theft. I would have had to pay out over $10,000 to creditors and $1.3 million plus interest for a house that I've never seen. I couldn't just look at my situation through my natural eyes, but I had to see if from a spiritual perspective. Although the "facts" said one thing, the Bible tells me that I shall know the truth and it shall make me free (*John 8:32*). While the "victim" in me would say, "I am defeated and won't be able to recover," the "victor" would respond, "I am more than a conqueror...I can do all things through Christ who strengthens me." I had to do like David in the Bible and encourage myself in the Lord. I was not alone because the Lord was walking through this process with me, and I know He will never leave or forsake me.

On the other hand, it's not unusual for identity theft to have a big emotional impact on you. In fact, you may feel anger, fear, helplessness, isolation, betrayal, rejection and even embarrassment. I can personally tell you that this traumatic crime can trigger deep fears regarding your financial security, personal safety and ability to trust people. However, in the midst of this crisis, you have to pull on your spiritual resources. Not only had the identity thief stolen my natural stuff, the real enemy was taking the opportunity to attack my spiritual identity. On the contrary, I was able to catch Satan in the act and demand that he immediately cease and desist. If you are going to stay on the road to recovery of your spiritual identity, you must decide whether you're going to be a victim or a victor. A victim gets victimized, but a victor has the victory. Which one do you prefer?

As you begin the process to get your stolen identity back, remember that the road to recovery is a journey, not a destination. You don't just arrive at the point of recovery, and then all of your problems are solved. It took me over four years from the time I discovered that my natural identity was stolen until I was able to fully recover from the nightmare. At that point, I couldn't say, "I finally recovered by identity, so I am done." I still had to continue to monitor my credit on a regular basis and take steps to protect my identity in the future. After I resolved the fraudulent bills with the creditors, then I had to deal with the mortgage companies to remove my name from the fraudulent house. When I thought the dilemma was over, I received a letter from the IRS regarding taxes on the house. Every time that I thought the ordeal was over, I had another hard blow. However, I had to make up my mind to persevere no matter what came my way. You must have the same attitude when it comes to recovering your spiritual identity. Be encouraged as you begin your road to recovery because this too shall pass in your life. The situation didn't come to stay, but it came to pass. Now, you're ready to go get the "real you" back.

TABLE 4
Indictment of Satan For Spiritual Identity Theft

**SUPREME COURT
OF THE KINGDOM OF HEAVEN**

INDICTMENT

<u>CASE NO.</u> 7777

**THE ALMIGHTY GOD ON BEHALF OF HIS CHILDREN,
PLAINTIFFS**

vs.

**SATAN (A/K/A THE DEVIL),
DEFENDANT**

COUNT 1

The said **SATAN (A/K/A THE DEVIL)**, hereinafter the **DEFENDANT**, is accused by the Grand Jury of the Kingdom of Heaven, by this Indictment for the crime of **SPIRITUAL IDENTITY THEFT**, in violation of **JOHN 10:10** in the **BIBLE**, a felony with a life-time sentence in hell, committed prior to the finding of this Indictment, and as follows:

On and about the time of his first appearance in the Garden of Eden until the filing of the subject charges, **DEFENDANT**, did unlawfully, intentionally, and knowingly **STEAL** (or attempted to do so) the **SPIRITUAL IDENTITY** of the **PLAINTIFFS**, without consent and with the intent to spiritually **KILL** and **DESTROY** them in the process.

SIGNED AND OFFICIALLY SEALED IN THE NAME OF:
Jesus Christ, The Advocate

Chapter 11

Go Get The "Real You" Back

Now that you know what you're entitled to recover as a "victor" of spiritual identity theft, it's time for you to go get the "real you" back. The key words are "go get" because the enemy is not going to hand over your identity without a fight. However, God will help you to recover everything that the enemy has stolen from you (your spiritual identity and all of the treasures tied to it), no matter how long it's been. To "recover" simply means to get something back. The Hebrew word for "recover" is "natsal," which literally means to snatch away. To "snatch" implies that you will grab something forcibly, rather than politely picking it up. To recover whatever you've lost, naturally and spiritually (whether it's your joy, peace, confidence, faith, job, health, or finances), you must take action to snatch those things back from the real enemy.

As discussed in Chapter 3, my computer crashed after it was attacked by a nasty virus earlier this year. I was desperate to try to recover my data files, so I contacted technical support for HP to get help. However, the tech told me that I needed to do a complete system restore and would lose all of my files. I just could not accept that response and called my webmaster. I asked him if there was any way that I could recover my files before I did the clean install. He told me to hold off and let him work on the computer for a couple of hours. He finally called and informed me that he had "fully" recovered all of my files and also backed them up for me. I refused to settle for a partial recovery of my system, losing my files in the process. I had to go to the right person who knew how to ensure my full recovery. Just because someone who didn't care about whether I recovered my stuff or not gave me a bad report, I did not have to accept it.

The same approach that I took to counter this natural attack needed to be applied to the spiritual attacks that I was going through. I needed to save and backup my "spiritual" hard drive with the Word of God to prevent any future attacks.

Likewise, when you are trying to recover your spiritual identity, you have to believe the report of the Lord about your full recovery. He doesn't want you to just get some of "you" back, but ALL of you (which is the real you who He created). Don't be moved by Satan or people who try to tell you that it's too late for you to recover ALL of your identity. Whose report are you going to believe? Remember that you are still in recovery mode, so the enemy is going to pull out all of the stops to get you to forfeit what belongs to you. He will try to bring up all of the bad reports from your past, even back to your childhood to get you to give up. You can't afford to be caught off guard when he reminds you of all the untrue things that your parents, spouse, siblings, friends, teachers or school counselor said during your life, such as "You'll never be anybody," "You're a failure," "Your best days are behind you," "You can't beat that addiction," "You're never going to get married or have children," "You're so stupid," "You'll always be an alcoholic," "You're going to get divorced like your parents," "You'll always be a single parent," "You know no one loves you," "You are not pretty enough," and of course, "You're just like your daddy." The list could go on and on, but the bottom line is you can only believe the report of the Lord. His report says,

> "If the Son therefore shall make you free, ye shall be free indeed."
>
> *John 8:36*

Once Jesus made you free, you were in fact free. This means that you are no longer in bondage, and no one or nothing can hold you back anymore. At this point, you have to recover ALL of the pieces of your identity that were stolen. Like in my dream where Satan only wanted to give me my wallet (a piece of my identity) back, he will also try to release yours in a piecemeal fashion when forced to do so. You can't accept anything less than your full spiritual identity. God also wants you to get back ALL of you, so you will have a "full" recovery. However, it's up to you to go snatch back everything that rightfully belongs to you.

You've Got The Power

Now it's time for you to prepare to go get your spiritual identity back, so you need to know that you've got the "power" to get your full recovery. The Lord would not send you into the enemy's camp without giving you the power to prevail over Satan. The Bible is clear on the type of power that we have when we're "in Christ."

> "Behold, I give unto you power to tread on serpents and scorpions, and over all the power of the enemy: and nothing shall by any means hurt you."
> *Luke 10:19*

In this verse, Jesus was responding to the seventy messengers that He had sent out to spread the gospel. They were excited that the demons had submitted to them in Jesus' name. Jesus reaffirmed to them that He had given them power to crush "serpents and scorpions" (figuratively referring to Satan) and over all the power of Satan. When Satan was cast out of heaven, his power was broken and he became subject to Jesus' authority. As a result, Satan could not harm them. What a powerful revelation of the "power" that we have in Jesus Christ.

We need to take a closer look at what the term, "power," means in *Luke 10:19*. The two Greek words for "power" are "dunamis" and "exusia." The term, "dunamis," denotes action and is the English word for "dynamite." It's the power that we receive from God. The other term, "exusia," denotes authority, which we receive from Jesus Christ. The latter term is referred to in verse 19. We receive the "dunamis" only in the measure in which we submit to the "exusia." Let me translate what that means..."You've got the power."

However, many of us know that we have the power (exusia) through Christ, but we are afraid to use it for some reason. We must walk in Christ's authority if we are going to go up against Satan. The enemy knows that you have the power, but he tries to make you doubt it when he steals your identity. It's time for you to take your power back from the enemy. For example, I know an elderly woman, Mrs. J., who also had the "power," but she didn't know it. Her husband used to take care of her until he passed away, and then she signed a power of attorney giving her relative, Ms. H, authority to handle all of her affairs, including her finances. Ms. H decided to sell Mrs. J's house and move her to a nursing home. However, Mrs. J, who was in her right mind, wanted to stay in her house. She pleaded with Ms. H to change her mind, but she refused. Mrs. J was so stressed out about having to move on short notice and wouldn't sleep or eat, but Ms. H kept moving forward with the plans for the nursing home to pick her up. When Mrs. J was wondering about what she could do, it dawned on her that Ms. H only had the power that Mrs. J had given her. Once she realized that she had the "real" power, she revoked the power of attorney and took back her power a few days before the planned move. Ms. H was furious because she no longer had the power over Mrs. J's affairs. Mrs. J had possessed the power the entire time, so all she had to do was take it back. This is the same way you have to do with Satan. He is a little slow, so you need to make sure he knows that "you've got the power." If you have, intentionally or accidentally, given the enemy a power of attorney over your affairs, it's time for you to revoke it effective immediately. The only One who should have a power of attorney over your life, including your spiritual identity, is God, so make sure you put the correct Agent with unlimited authority in your new document.

At this point, you know that you have the power, so why are you not using it? You can't be shy or polite when you're dealing with the enemy. I always say that you can't patty-cake the devil. You have to be persistent and can't take "no" for an answer. Satan has to release your identity, period. You need to give your spiritual identity crisis or amnesia an expiration date, effective immediately.

We can learn a lot about persistence from the parable of the widow and the unjust judge in *Luke 18*.

> "And there was a widow in that city; and she came unto him, saying, Avenge me of mine adversary. And he would not for a while: but afterward he said within himself, Though I fear not God, nor regard man; Yet because this widow troubleth me, I will avenge her, lest by her continual coming she weary me."
>
> *Luke 18:3-5*

In this scripture, Jesus introduces this unnamed widow, who went to an unjust judge who didn't fear God and demanded that he give her justice against her adversary. We don't know how the widow was being cheated, but the judge appeared to be on her opponent's side and would not give her justice. However, the widow kept going back to the judge and wouldn't take "no" for an answer. Instead, every time that the court was in session, she was there demanding the justice to which she was entitled. She knew that the squeaky wheel gets the oil, but the judge refused her demands for a long time. In the end, she bothered him to the point that she wore him down, and he finally gave her the justice she sought.

Jesus later told the audience how the parable applied to them. If an unjust judge will see that justice is done in response to persistent requests from the widow, how much more will a just God do to bring justice to His own beloved people who pray constantly for relief? How badly do you want your identity back? Are you willing to be as persistent and demanding as the widow was to get it back? If so, you are ready to go into the enemy's camp. Follow me.

Take It All Back

Once you know the power that you have in Christ, all that's left to do is to take ALL of your "stuff" back from the enemy. "ALL" means everything that Satan has stolen from you, not just your spiritual identity. As you know, you're going to have to seize your stuff by "force."

> "And from the days of John the Baptist until now the kingdom of heaven suffereth violence, and the violent take it by force."
>
> *Matthew 11:12*

Since there is a violent attack against the kingdom of God, as believers, we need to be violent in return. In other words, we have to be forceful when confronting the invisible forces that are warring against us. We have to be prepared to fight in the battle under God's direction and violently come against the enemy. You are now at the point of no return, so you have to move forward and be ready to use force to take back what belongs to you.

Are you ready to go get the "real you" back? The enemy is not going to voluntarily give your identity back, so you will have to snatch it from him. When you seek

God concerning your spiritual identity, He will let you know when to go after it and give you peace about your full recovery. We can learn a few lessons from David, who pursued his enemy and recovered all before he took the throne as king of Israel.

When the Philistines were about to go into battle with the Israelites before the death of King Saul, David and his men returned to Ziklag. David discovered that the Amalekites had burned the town and carried off his wives, the other women and their property. While he was gone, the "enemy" had come and stolen his stuff. David was greatly distressed because his men threatened to stone him. He had to encourage himself in the Lord (*1 Samuel 30:6*), and that's exactly what we have to do. Then, David consulted the Lord before he moved forward to pursue his enemy, and He responded, "Pursue: for thou shalt surely overtake them, and without fail recover all" (*1 Samuel 30:8*). Not only did God tell him to pursue his enemy, He assured him of the victory and the "full recovery" of his stuff. David and his men obeyed God and went after and defeated the Amalekites. They recovered all of their families and property like God said he would.

When God tells you to pursue the enemy that stole your identity, you already have the victory before the battle. It's a fixed fight because the battle is not yours, but the Lord's.

> "Ye shall not need to fight in this battle: set yourselves, stand ye still, and see the salvation of the LORD with you..."
>
> 2 Chronicles 20:17

In this scripture, King Jehoshaphat was about to go into battle with the Moabites and the Ammonites. God told him that he would not have to fight, but to watch Him save him from his enemies. Similarly, it's awesome that God allows us to hold our peace, and He fights our battles for us. All we need to do is to stand still and see the salvation of the Lord. We also must step out and obey what God tells us to do, and He will do the rest.

Like Satan did with Job, he is after our spiritual identity and wants to ruin our relationship with God. When God allowed Satan to test Job, He allowed him to take his health, children and his material possessions as long as his life was spared. After he lost everything, Job still held on to his spiritual identity.

> "...And said, Naked came I out of my mother's womb, and naked shall I return thither: the LORD gave, and the LORD hath taken away; blessed be the name of the LORD."
>
> *Job 1:21*

Satan even used Job's wife and friends to try to get him to curse God, but he refused to do so. It's interesting that he lost everything, except his faithless wife. If his identity was tied to "natural" things, he would have had a hard time not giving in to defeat when he lost everything.

> "And the LORD turned the captivity of Job, when he prayed for his friends: also the LORD gave Job twice as much as he had before."
>
> *Job 42:10*

After Job suffered a tragic loss, God gave him twice as much as he previously had. As my grandmother, My-My, used to say, "God gave him double for his trouble" because he held on. When God allowed Satan to try to steal Job's spiritual identity, He already knew that Job would not forfeit it and ensured that he received a full recovery of everything that he lost. The Lord will do the same for you if you just hold on to your identity, no matter how bad things get in your life.

Even though your stuff may be in the enemy's hands, it still belongs to you. Your spiritual identity belongs to you, so ask God to restore all that you've lost. When the enemy takes your stuff, it's just like having locusts and worms eat up your good crops. In the book of Joel, God promised to reverse the destructive impact of the insects.

> "And I will restore to you the years that the locust hath eaten, the cankerworm, and the caterpillar, and the palmerworm, my great army which I sent among you."
>
> *Joel 2:25*

Here, God promised to restore the Israelites' crops, which had been devoured by the pesky locusts and worms. God is in the restoration business, so let Him give you the joy, peace, strength, power, finances or whatever you've lost back. After He restores those things, you will also experience a full recovery of your spiritual identity. Once you get the "real" you back, you need to let go of the "fake" one.

Will The "Real You" Stand Up?

Once you get your spiritual identity back from the enemy, you can finally discover the "real" you. To "discover" means to uncover something that is already there, but it may be unknown. Your "real" identity was there all of the time once you put your trust in Christ, so all you had to do was uncover it. Just because you couldn't see your identity doesn't mean that it was not there. The "real you" is who God created you to be from the inside out, and it's time for the real you to stand up for the world to see.

If you have found the "real" you, have you wondered what happened to the "fake" you, which is the edited version of who you were supposed to be? As stated in Chapter 2, when your natural identity is stolen, you have in effect been duplicated. Then, there are two of you walking around, the "fake" you and the "real" you. Just like the creditors couldn't figure out which one of you to believe, the same thing holds true with your spiritual identity. When Satan steals your real identity, he replaces it with a fake one that looks and sounds just like you. However, the only one who can automatically recognize the real you when He sees it is God, even when you can't. He can spot the clone of you from a mile away, but what about you?

Would you know the "real" you if you were standing right in front of you? When you have spent more time with the "fake" you, it may not be as easy to tell as you think. It's like looking at identical twins and not being able to tell the difference between the two. The real you and the fake you may look the same on the outside, but the real difference is in the inside. Even you may have to look really close to recognize the real you, and others may not know the difference at all.

This tug of war between the real and fake you reminds me of the story of Jacob when he prepared to return home to Canaan after 20 years. When he deceitfully stole his brother's natural identity, Jacob had traded in his own spiritual identity and had been wrestling with who he was ever since. The name, Jacob, means, "supplanter," and he had chosen to live his life as a trickster (the fake him) for years. However, God already knew the "real" him when He told his mother that Esau would serve Jacob while they were both in her womb. When Jacob was ready to get his "real" identity back, he had to wrestle with an angel of the Lord all night until the morning.

> "And Jacob was left alone; and there wrestled a man with him until the breaking of the day. And when he saw that he prevailed not against him, he touched the hollow of his thigh; and the hollow of Jacob's thigh was out of joint, as he wrestled with him. And he said, Let me go, for the day breaketh. And he said, I will not let thee go, except thou bless me."
>
> *Genesis 32:24-26*

While Jacob was wrestling (hand-to-hand combat) with the angel, he was also having an "internal" struggle between the "fake" him (who he had become) and the "real" him (who God created him to be). He couldn't even recognize the "real" Him until he had a personal encounter with God. Jacob thought he was winning the fight, but the angel touched his thigh and knocked it out of joint. The Lord had to break him, so he could get a breakthrough. Once God revealed who Jacob really was, he would not let go until he received his full blessing. He was not looking for more wealth or possessions, but his spiritual identity. After Jacob discovered his "real" identity, God gave him a new name, "Israel," which means "he who struggles with God." His new name signified his new identity and that he finally knew who he really was, so his struggle was over. He was not blessed based on *what* he was holding, but *who* he was holding (God). The fake Jacob laid down in the fight, but the real one (Israel) stood up. Likewise, it's time for the real you to stand up and walk into the "new."

Chapter 12

Walk Into The "New"

Now that you have fully recovered your stolen identity and discovered the "real you," it's time for you to walk into the "new." I know it's been a long and challenging process for you, but it's not quite over yet. Now that you know who God created you to be, you have to embrace your "new" identity (the real you). As a result, you no longer have to pick up the "fake" you because it's a part of your past. Believe it or not, getting your spiritual identity back was the easy part, but the critical test is whether you can keep it. Now that you have your identity back, you need to hold on to it with a bulldog grip to keep it out of the reach of the enemy. In order to do so, you have to start walking into the "new," which means dealing with something that has just been found or discovered.

As you walk into all of the "new" in your life, it's essential that you let go of the old. You need to keep your eyes on the "new" things in front of you, rather than focusing on the "old" things that are behind you.

> "Brethren, I count not myself to have apprehended: but this one thing I do, forgetting those things which are behind, and reaching forth unto those things which are before, I press toward the mark for the prize of the high calling of God in Christ Jesus."
> *Philippians 3:13-14*

In this scripture, Paul was emphasizing the necessity of forgetting the past things that can't be changed, which includes the issues related to the old you. He was encouraging the people to keep their focus on the "prize" awaiting them in the future. It's difficult to embrace your future if you keep dwelling on your past. It's time to let go of the "old" and to get ready to walk into your "new season."

A "New" Season

In Chapter 1 of my book, *Willing to Wait*, I talked about when I began to walk into a "new" season in my life several years ago. Initially, I had several dreams about driving a new car and walking into a new house, but I didn't know what they meant. As I began to walk into that new season, I began to move by "revelation" rather than by what I felt or thought. When God first revealed the "new" things in my life, I was a little hesitant about taking any action. However, once I heard His clear directions, I walked into those blessings without any reservations. He was waiting for me to surrender my will and to say "yes" to the new season. As a result, I entered into a season of sudden changes in my life, where I received a promotion at work, a new

Walk Into The "New"

car and a new house in three consecutive weeks. Only the Lord could orchestrate a series of blessings like that so suddenly. I called the experience my "season of suddenlies." God will lead you into the "new" to ensure you're at the "right" place at the "right" time. You can trust whatever God has revealed to you because He is doing a "new thing" in your life.

> "Remember ye not the former things, neither consider the things of old. Behold, I will do a new thing; now it shall spring forth; shall ye not know it? I will even make a way in the wilderness, and rivers in the desert."
>
> *Isaiah 43:18-19*

You have to decide not to look back to the old things because eventually you will turn back. God wants to do a new thing in you, so all you have to do is surrender to His will. However, the enemy will try to get you to return to your "old" life, but you have to keep moving forward in your new season.

The closer I got to the completion of this book, the real enemy stepped up his attack against me. He sent all kinds of distractions and obstacles to try to hinder me, but he didn't succeed. I was getting hit on every side, at work, at home and in relationships. However, I knew that no weapon that was formed against me would prosper (Isaiah 54:17). I could sense that a "shifting" was taking place in my life, and the enemy didn't want me to go to the next level in God. When I prayed about this "new" season in my life, the Lord spoke that it was time for me to "walk into the new." I was excited about the "new," but I didn't have the full revelation yet. The Lord knows that I am a visual person, so He always shows me things in the natural first. Then, He will give me the full spiritual understanding later.

Suddenly, all of the "things" around me started to break without any explanation. I would try to do a "quick fix" on the things because it would take too long to figure out what was actually wrong. However, it was just a matter of time before the "old" things had to be replaced with "new" ones. It started with my car having unexpected problems with the fuel pump, and the dealership had to replace the part less than a year after I bought it. I was not happy with the replacement, but I settled for it because they told me that the problem was fixed. However, I continued to have problems, so I had to elevate the situation to the right people and remember that I had the "power." I faxed a detailed letter to the General Manager with my concerns on a Friday afternoon, and I picked out my brand new car on the following Thursday.

Before I could get my new car, I had to release the old one and begin walking into the new. Then, I started doing an inventory of all of the old items that had to be replaced with new ones in a short period of time, including: 1) my computer desk, 2) my printer, 3) my blackberry, 4) my cell phone, 5) my answering machine and 6) my headset. The technicians tried to fix each of these things, but they all stopped working completely a couple of days later. I didn't even have to request a new one of the items because the technician told me that I needed a "new" one. My response was, "Okay." After I received all the "new" things, I noticed that my whole mindset changed about settling for the old stuff that didn't work properly. I began to proclaim to myself, "I am walking in the new." Several people asked me how I was getting all of these "new" things, particularly since their "request" for the same new items had been turned down. All I could say was, "Favor is not fair! God is good!" When God told me to "walk into the new," He meant literally.

When you get something new, the typical response should be to get rid of the old version. However, sometimes the old thing is more comfortable, so you continue to use it. For example, you may buy a new pair of shoes, but keep wearing the old ones. It's easier to keep the shiny, new ones in the box because they will have to be broken in. In the meantime, you would continue to wear the old ones and keep prolonging stepping into the new. Before you know it, the new shoes have been sitting in your closet for a year while the soles are coming off the old ones. Similarly, you may know that it's time for you to walk into the "new" in your life, but you have continued to settle for your old ways. Once you have the "new you" back, you should be ready to receive all of the other "new" things that the Lord has in store for you.

When God confirms that you're walking into a "new season," you can rest assured that you are in the right place at the right time. There is a pre-determined "season" for every thing that happens in your life.

> "To every thing there is a season, and a time to every purpose under the heaven:"
> *Ecclesiastes 3:1*

King Solomon proclaimed that every "thing" has a season, and there's a time for every purpose. He observed that God had pre-programmed every activity of life into His spiritual computer to happen at some point in time and to last for a certain duration. King Solomon implied that there is a cycle of life, which has a circular recurrence of the same events. Since only God knows the timing of your new season, you have to rely on Him to reveal it to you at the appointed time.

If you are serious about walking into the "new," you have to choose to let go of the old. The old and the new are like oil and water, and they don't mix very well. If you inherited a new house that was fully furnished, you wouldn't bring all of your old furniture with you. What God is saying is if you can let go of the old things, He can release the new things that He has for you. However, you can't hold on to the new and the old at the same time.

> "No man putteth a piece of new cloth unto an old garment, for that which is put in to fill it up taketh from the garment, and the rent is made worse. Neither do men put new wine into old bottles: else the bottles break, and the wine runneth out, and the bottles perish: but they put new wine into new bottles, and both are preserved."
> *Matthew 9:16-17*

Here, Jesus gave two different illustrations with the same meaning on the dangers of mixing the old with the new. This is an important message that has direct application to our lives today. In response to the question about why His disciples did not fast, Jesus first uses the example of an old garment tearing and needing a patch. If you use a piece of new cloth on the old garment, it will shrink. When it does shrink, it pulls the threads and makes a worse tear than you had before. He was saying that God is doing a "new thing" in Christ. Jesus confirmed that He did not come to destroy the old law, but to fulfill it. Now in Christ, God is doing a new thing…salvation by grace contrasted with the law which could never save. Jesus was radically new and completely different. Your whole life can be made new in Jesus Christ.

Then, Jesus provided a second example of trying to put "new wine" into old wine skins. In those days, animal skins were used to keep wine. When they were new, they were elastic and would stretch to hold the wine. As the skins aged, they became brittle. If new wine were put into the old wine skins as it fermented and expanded, the skins would burst. There were no old rituals which could contain the new wine that Jesus offered. They were useless containers for God's new work in Christ. God's purpose was to bring in something new, and you should be walking into the new when your identity is in Christ. Not only are you walking in a new season, but you also have been given a new name.

A "New" Name

Once we know who we are in Christ and are walking in our new identity, we need to know the significance of our "new" name. When parents find out that they are expecting a baby, one important decision for them to make is what to name their child. There are various ways they can come up with the right name, such as buying a book on names or selecting a favorite name, a relative's name or a celebrity's name. Regardless of how they come up with the name, the reality is that their child will be identified based on that name. So, what does a name have to do with our identity?

Your name has a lot to do with your identity and can actually have a big influence on it. When I was growing up, I didn't like my first name because kids would tease me about it. I looked up what it meant when I was older and realized that it fits me exactly. The name "DeMonica" means "advisor of," which is what I am always doing. I had never met anyone with my name, so I thought I was the only one with it until I met several women with my name, some of whom were older than me. When I signed up for Facebook, I was surprised to receive friend requests from five women named, "DeMonica." We had a group discussion about how we got our names and were shocked to discover the similarities in our personalities and how our names fit us so perfectly. We even had mutual friends, who never said that they knew another "DeMonica."

When it comes to identity theft, remember that the key part of your identity is your name. All of the other personal information and numbers stem from your name. As a result, your name can sometimes be used to your detriment and may have to be changed to protect you from criminals. In 1970, the U.S. government established the federal Witness Protection Program to address this issue. The program still provides a new identity to people who testify in court as witnesses for the prosecution against criminals who may have threatened their lives. In exchange for their testimony, the government gives those witnesses completely new identities, which usually include new names.

Likewise, God promises His redeemed a "new name."

> "...and thou shalt be called by a new name, which the mouth of the LORD shall name."
>
> *Isaiah 62:2*

God has given each of His children a "new" name and identity in Christ, who is the head of His spiritual Witness Protection Program that protects believers who testify on His behalf. This identity replaces the one Satan offered Adam and Eve in the Garden of Eden when he tried to steal their identities as children of God. Christ paid the ultimate price with His blood to provide us with this new identity. That's why we belong to God and are no longer our own.

> "For ye are bought with a price: therefore glorify God in your body, and in your spirit, which are God's."
>
> *1 Corinthians 6:20*

Now that you know you have a new name and identity in Christ, let me ask you the same question from Chapter 4: "Who do you think you are?" Well, you are a child of the King and belong to Him. As a believer, your salvation is all about getting a new identity, so all you need to do is walk into who you are. Once you discover your "real identity," you can help others who don't know Christ or have had their identities stolen to find theirs. The more you tell people who they are in God, the more willing they will be to become His servants. When they start saying who they think they are, you can tell them who God says they really are. Then, they can discover what it means to find their identity in Christ, like you did.

Instead of buying into who the enemy or world says we are, we must start believing what the Word says about us as we walk into the new. However, if you don't know what God's Word has to say, you will easily be persuaded to become what the enemy tells you. At this point, you don't want to give Satan the ammunition to use against you. Whatever your area of weakness or your past is, God has given you a new name if you are in Christ. Contrary to what the world might say, you are also not defined by what you do for a living, where you live or what kind of car you drive.

Remember how God took a lowly shepherd boy, David, and called him a king. What about the chief persecutor of the church, Saul, whom He called an apostle? He also took a prideful fisherman, Simon Peter, and made him "the rock" upon which Christ would build His church. What the world calls an outcast or misfit, God will give a new name and a change of identity.

Don't you know that God is in the business of changing names? All through the Bible are examples of when God changed a person's name because there was a change in the direction of their lives: 1) Abram became Abraham, which means the "father of many nations;" 2) Sarai became Sarah, which means "princess;" 3) Jacob became Israel, which means "struggled with God;" and 4) Saul became Paul, which means "small." Likewise, God has changed your name to match your new identity.

Since you have a new name, you must be careful about what you call yourself and which name you answer to. When I was growing up and even now, I heard Christians say, "I am just a sinner saved by grace." If the Bible says we're "saints," why do some believers still identify with being a "sinner?"

> "To all that be in Rome, beloved of God, called to be saints: Grace to you and peace from God our Father, and the Lord Jesus Christ."
> *Romans 1:7*

Here, I think Paul addressed the church as "saints" because he hoped they would answer to that name. If he talked to them as if they were saints, they would start acting more like saints. If you always see yourself as a sinner, you'll be in spiritual bondage. You've got to see yourself as free and redeemed. Are you trying to be free, or has the Lord already made you free? God tells us that we are "saints," but many believers still see themselves as "sinners saved by grace." Is being a "sinner" your scriptural identity? No, it's not because God doesn't call you a sinner, but a saint. You were a sinner before you accepted Christ. If you still think of yourself as a sinner, guess what you will do? You'll live like a sinner. Why not identify yourself with who you really are, a saint who may occasionally sin, but has been redeemed by the blood of Christ. When I see believers not acting as if they believe this truth, I ask the question, "Are we dealing with the saints or the aints"? You decide.

Now that you know your new name, how do you identify with Christ? Do you have some of His characteristics? Do you talk or act like Him? The Bible says that you will know a tree by its fruit (*Matthew 7:16-17*). If you are a lemon tree, people should see lemons hanging from you. If you are in Christ, people should see Christ in your life. You have to allow the Holy Spirit to lead you, and let the life of Christ be seen in the way you live. This is why Satan tries so hard to steal your identity. He rejoices when people do not know you from anyone else, and of course when you don't know who you are. If you are a chameleon and just blend into your surroundings, he doesn't see you as a threat. You can walk around with your Bible and put fish decals on your car, but your identity has been lost if the world doesn't see Christ in your life somehow. The world doesn't need more Christians, but they just need to see the "real" ones.

It's a shame if you have a new name, but are unaware of your rightful treasures when you walk into the new. However, that's exactly what happens with many believers who live without taking advantage of God's promises of joy, peace, rest, strength, love and other spiritual treasures, which they are entitled to because of their new identity in Christ. What treasures is God holding in trust for you to claim?

A "New" Walk

Now that you know your new name, you have to understand what it means to have a "new walk." To "walk" means to move over a surface by taking steps at a slower pace than a run, which means that action is required for you to get from point A to point B. Many of us may be aware of who we are in Christ, but we have not started walking into our new identity yet. In other words, we have not taken any action to move toward our new life. The Word tells us to "walk" into the newness of life.

> "Therefore we are buried with him by baptism into death: that like as Christ was raised up from the dead by the glory of the Father, even so we also should walk in newness of life."
>
> *Romans 6:4*

In this scripture, the apostle Paul reaffirms when we put our trust in Christ, we are not only crucified with Him, but we are also resurrected with Him. Once our standing changed with God, we were enabled to also "walk in newness of life."

It's not enough to just have a new life, but it's necessary that you continue to walk in it. Walking requires some effort on your part, which means you have to exert some energy. Additionally, walking implies that there's a destination or goal in mind. When a person walks, he or she is moving purposefully to accomplish something, whether it is to get some exercise or to go to the store. God requires that we "walk in newness of life," which is also purposeful. When we walk in the new, we can't just aimlessly shuffle through life with no direction. We can rest assured that we are headed somewhere, like the Israelites were moving toward the Promised Land.

One of my favorite biblical examples of someone who had to learn to "walk into the new" is the man at the pool of Bethesda. He was in a new season in his life, but like many of us, he had not walked into it yet.

> "And a certain man was there, which had an infirmity thirty and eight years. When Jesus saw him lie, and knew that he had been now a long time in that case, he saith unto him, Wilt thou be made whole?... Jesus saith unto him, Rise, take up thy bed, and walk. And immediately the man was made whole, and took up his bed, and walked: and on the same day was the sabbath."
>
> *John 5:5-6, 8-9*

Similar to this man, the Lord wants us to be whole, physically, mentally, emotionally and spiritually when we receive our new identity. However, we are usually good at making excuses for why we haven't crossed over to the new yet. In the above scripture, there was a certain man at the pool of Bethseda who had been afflicted for thirty-eight years. If the man stepped into the pool when the water was stirred, he could be healed from whatever disease he had. This man desired to be healed and to walk in the new, but he kept making excuses for why he couldn't. When Jesus asked the man, "Wilt thou be made whole?" he responded with two excuses: 1) he didn't have anyone to put him in the pool, and 2) other people would get in front of him when he tried. The real problem was that the man was looking for someone else to do for him what he could do for himself.

Jesus told the man to do three essential things, which required action on his part, in order to walk into the new. First, the man had to "rise," which literally meant the man had to get up out of his current situation. As long as he stayed where he was, he would continue in his old ways. Standing up signified that he was no longer trying to deal with his situation lying down. Second, he had to "take up thy bed," which implied that after he got up, he had to get rid of the old crutches that he was relying on. He had to get out of his comfort zone to experience his "new" life. The bed represented the obstacles that had been hindering him from getting his healing. Finally, he had to "walk," which signifies that he was ready to go into a new direction in his life. He could no longer just talk about where he wanted to go, but he had to put one foot in front of the other to walk into his new destiny.

After the man obeyed Jesus, he was immediately made whole. The thing (the bed) that had been carrying him, he was now carrying it. Likewise, you have to move while the waters are troubled, so you can receive your full recovery. It's time for you to pick up your own bed and walk. Get up and stop waiting for someone to do for you what you can do for yourself. I have one question for you, "Will you be made whole?" If so, you have to choose to embrace your "new walk" and move in the direction that God has ordained for your life. He wants you to be healed, delivered and set free in every area of your life. God wants you to reclaim who you are in Christ and to rebuild your life base on your "real" identity.

A "New" You

While you continue to walk into the new, you have to embrace the "new you." At the beginning of each year, you likely hear everyone talking about their New Year's resolutions. So, it's common for your family and friends to expect the "new you" to show up in the "new year." However, once you have your "real" identity back, the "new you" can debut today. You don't have to wait for the New Year because you're already walking into the new today. You may not look different on the outside, but your perception of who you think you are should have changed. When the old saints got saved, they used to say the following about their salvation experience, "I looked at my hands and they looked new...I looked at my feet and they did too." In other words, their hands and feet didn't physically change, but their perception of who they thought they were had changed. For example, you may have had an "old" problem with your weight and didn't like how you looked before, but you should see yourself differently when you're walking into the new, whether you lose weight or not. From the outside, you may look exactly the same, but who you really are is based on who you are in the inside. Moreover, you should see yourself differently now because this is the "new you."

A similar example is when Jesus healed the blind man at Bethsaida.

> "And he took the blind man by the hand, and led him out of the town; and when he had spit on his eyes, and put his hands upon him, he asked him if he saw ought. And he looked up, and said, I see men as trees, walking. After that he put his hands again upon his eyes, and made him look up: and he was restored; and saw every man clearly."
>
> Mark 8:23-25

When Jesus and His disciples arrived in Bethsaida, some people brought a blind man to Him for healing.

However, Jesus led the man outside the village, which was one exception to His public ministry. When Jesus spit on the man's eyes and put His hand on them, it activated the man's faith. At first the healing was only "partial" because the man looked up and could see people, but they looked like trees moving around. Jesus asked the man a rhetorical question about what he could see. The man was no longer totally blind, but his sight was not fully restored. Then, Jesus, put His hands on the man's eyes again. His sight was restored, and he began to see everything clearly. Now his sight was perfect. Likewise, we need to keep checking our sight until we know that we are seeing our "new" self the same way that God does. At that point, you can finally say that you've discovered the real you, so all you need to do is walk in your new life.

Case Studies: Walking Into New Lives

The following case studies are real-life examples of men and women who experienced a spiritual identity crisis and allowed the enemy to steal their spiritual identities in the process. All of them are believers, but they allowed their identities to become tied to an unreliable source after experiencing a difficult situation in their lives. Some of them knew that something was missing in their lives, but they didn't know how to fill the void. At that point, they made a decision to do a personal inventory of their lives to fully understand their real identity in Christ. Now, they are on the road to recover their stolen identities and have started to walk into the new. As a result, they now have a "new life" in Christ and have committed to the ongoing process to hold on to their real identities.

1) ***Case Study No. 1 - "Who am I if I'm not married?"***
This woman was a single parent who had never been married. Her father was not around when she was growing up, so she desired for her child to have a father in his life. She was desperate to get married because she didn't feel "complete" without a man in her life. She dealt with the fear of rejection all of her life and was constantly looking for "Mr. Right" to fill her void. When she met the so-called man of her dreams, she saw the signs of his control issues but chose to overlook them. Despite the many warnings, she rushed into marrying him, and he physically and mentally abused her. She lost her faith, confidence and self-esteem in the process. *Now, she has fully recovered her spiritual identity in Christ and is enjoying being single again. She has a closer relationship with God and her child and is focused on fulfilling her purpose.*

2) ***Case Study No. 2 - "Who am I if I'm divorced?"***
This man got married at a young age and had children. His father was not a part of his life when he was young, so he struggled with his identity for years. As a result, he worked hard to make a name for himself and was a well-respected community leader. He had issues with being alone, which was the key reason he got married. He had major problems in his marriage, but he pretended that everything was going well. He didn't believe in divorce, so he was mentally and emotionally devastated when his wife left him. After his divorce, he began to doubt himself and felt like he was a failure. He didn't trust women anymore and knew that he needed to be healed from this painful situation. *Now, he has reclaimed his real identity and has addressed the*

issues that he had dealt with during his divorce. He is still active in the community and is walking in his God-given purpose. He has remarried for the right reason and is enjoying spending time with his family.

3) **Case Study No. 3 - "Who am I if I can't have kids?"** This woman was very focused on her education and career. She was in an abusive relationship in college, which damaged her self-esteem. She was a very attractive person on the outside, but she didn't feel that way on the inside. She later married the man of her dreams and wanted to have kids right away. After having several miscarriages, she was finally able to carry her last child to full term. However, her child was still born, and she was unable to have any more kids because of other complications. She was devastated about not being able to experience motherhood. The woman and her husband were later able to adopt a child, and she felt fulfilled temporarily. After several years, she went through a mid-life crisis and left her husband. Since she had never fully recovered from the loss of several kids, she was trying to fill a void in her life. *Now, after much soul-searching, she has found herself and got her confidence back. She is enjoying spending time with herself and her kids and is focused on embracing her new life.*

4) **Case Study No. 4 - "Who am I if I lose a loved one?"** This man was one of five siblings and was the next to the youngest child. His siblings were much older than him, so he was closer to his younger brother. His stepfather was an alcoholic and verbally abusive to his mother, his siblings

and him. He would tell him that he would not do anything with his life, so the man dealt with the fear of failure. The man left college and moved far away from home to start a new career, and he was very successful. However, the week before he returned home, his younger brother committed suicide. The man felt guilty and blamed himself for not being there for his brother. He started drinking to dull the pain and struggled with depression, and his life began to spin out of control. *Now, he has surrendered his life to God and decided to confront the unresolved issues in his life. He has embraced who he was created to be and has gotten his life back on track. He is happily married and has two children.*

5) **Case Study No. 5 - "Who am I if I change my appearance?"** The woman was told that she was overweight all of her life. She was used to being teased as a child by her family and peers about her weight, and her life's goal was to be a size 8. After trying all kinds of diets, she decided to get a tummy tuck. She lost a lot of weight initially, but she still didn't like how she looked. When she looked in the mirror, she still saw herself as fat. She became depressed and would overeat to feel better, but it would only make her sick. She felt helpless and unloved. *Now, after finally dealing with her issue with rejection and self-hatred, she has accepted herself for who she is on the inside. She is happy with her appearance because she realized who she was created to be. She got married to a man who loved her just the way she is.*

6) **Case Study No. 6 - *"Who am I if I'm struggling with my finances?"*** This woman got married young and didn't have much at that time. During her marriage, she has struggled financially for years. After her husband got sick, she became the main provider for her family. The pressure and stress had begun to affect her health. She was constantly applying for loans to pay off her credit cards bills, but they got maxed out again as soon as she paid them off. She spent most of her time trying to figure out how to get more money to pay the bills. She had a void in her life and had been trying to fill it with things. *Now, she is looking to God as her provider and trusting Him to supply her needs. Once she realized that who she is was not based on her finances, she began to embrace her spiritual identity. She is working with her husband to manage their finances and desires to be a good steward over everything God has blessed her with.*

After reading the above case studies, you should have a good idea about how your identity can be stolen in various areas, which mostly tie back to the 3 P's in Chapter 8. However, the good news is that you can still receive a full recovery of your real identity. All you have to do is walk into the new and reclaim who God has created you to be. Now that you have discovered your real identity, what are you going to do with it? All I can tell you is to continue to "walk into the new!"

STEP 4
Review Questions

1) Do you expect to receive a "full recovery" of your stolen spiritual identity? What would you consider to be a "full recovery" (be specific)? Would you settle for a partial recovery for any reason? If so, for what reasons?

2) On the road to recovery of your "real" identity, did you know what you were entitled to as a follower of Christ? If so, specify and explain what you're entitled to.

3) Do you still consider yourself to be a "victim" of spiritual identity theft? Why or Why not? Or do you see yourself as a "victor?" If so, how did you move from a victim to a victor? Explain in detail.

4) Have you gotten the "real you" back yet? Were you prepared to confront the enemy to get it back? How long was the process? How did it affect you naturally and spiritually?

5) What does it mean to "walk" into the new? What three essential things are required? Have you embraced the new season in your life? If so, explain how (be specific)?

6) Have you found the "new you?" Does the "new you" look anything like the "old" you? If not, what are the differences? What steps can you take to hold on to the new you?

ABOUT THE AUTHOR

DeMonica D. Gladney is an attorney in the Houston, Texas area. She received her Bachelor of Science degree in Criminal Justice, *cum laude*, from Lamar University and her Jurisprudence Doctorate, *cum laude*, from the University of Houston Law Center. Ms. Gladney is currently Counsel for Exxon Mobil Corporation and previously served as a Briefing Attorney for the Texas Fourteenth Court of Appeals.

Ms. Gladney is the personification of commitment and excellence. She is the Chair of the Women Lawyers Division and Corporate Liaison for the Commercial Law Section of the National Bar Association (NBA) and received the 2008 and 2010 NBA Presidential Award. Ms. Gladney is a former President of the Houston Lawyers Association and Chair of the African American Lawyers Section of the State Bar of Texas. She is a member of the Houston Bar Association, the Corporate Counsel Women of Color and Alpha Kappa Alpha Sorority, Inc. She was selected for the 2010 Who's Who Among Executives and Professionals and the Who's Who in Black Houston.

In addition to a successful legal career, Ms. Gladney is an inspiring and accomplished writer and poet. She is the bestselling author of the books, *Identity Theft: Discovering the Real You*, *Willing to Wait: From Revelation to Manifestation*, and *Reflections from God*. Her book, *Willing to Wait*, was ranked #7 on the BCBD National Independent Publishers' Top 50 Bestseller's List.

Ms. Gladney is a highly sought after inspirational speaker and has been featured on the Daystar TV Network - Houston Celebration Show and in the Pearland Journal and Ladies First Magazine as well as on various radio talk shows around the country.

CONTACT THE AUTHOR

To schedule a speaking engagement or book signing, contact her at:

DeMonica D. Gladney, Esq.
P.M.B. #227
8325 Broadway, #202
Pearland, TX 77581
Email: info@authordemonicadgladney.com

Visit her online at:

www.authordemonicadgladney.com

Connect with her at:

www.facebook.com/dgladney
www.twitter.com/dgladney
www.willingtowait.wordpress.com/

OTHER BOOKS BY THE AUTHOR

Willing to Wait:
From Revelation to Manifestation
(ISBN: 978-0-9724229-2-5)

Willing to Wait is a practical and insightful guide for those who are frustrated or impatient about being in God's "waiting" room. Not only does **Willing to Wait** show you "how" to wait, it walks you step-by-step through the waiting process that we all must go through in preparation for receiving God's blessings. **Willing to Wait** is a must-read for those who have chosen to wait on God and are searching for the spiritual tools to empower them while they wait.

Available at:
www.demonicagladney.com
www.amazon.com
www.barnesandnoble.com

OTHER BOOKS BY THE AUTHOR

Reflections From God
(ISBN: 978-0-9724229-0-1)

Reflections from God is a powerful and innovative collection of poems arranged around major themes such as faith, life, love and mothers as reflected through the eyes of God. **Reflections from God** gives new meaning to the importance of having spiritual insight into the many changes and challenges that we face in everyday life.

Available at:
www.demonicagladney.com
www.amazon.com
www.barnesandnoble.com

OTHER SUGGESTED BOOKS

INDENTITY THEFT

Author:

Mari J. Frank, Esq.
(www.MariFrank.com)
(www.identitytheft.org)

The Complete Idiot's Guide To Recovering From Identity Theft

From Victim To Victor: A Step By Step Guide For Ending The Nightmare Of Identity Theft

Safeguard Your Identity: Protect Yourself With A Personal Privacy Audit

IDENTITY RECOVERY

Author:

Dr. Connie Stewart
Life Coach, Life in Bloom
(www.lifeinbloom.org)

The Master Orchestrator